Jump-Start Your Canine Care

Jump-Start Your Canine Care

Doggie Basics

V. NUNLEY

iUniverse, Inc.
Bloomington

Jump-Start Your Canine Care
Doggie Basics

iUniverse books may be ordered through booksellers or by contacting:

iUniverse
1663 Liberty Drive
Bloomington, IN 47403
www.iuniverse.com
1-800-Authors (1-800-288-4677)

ISBN: 978-1-4620-6019-1 (sc)
ISBN: 978-1-4620-6021-4 (hc)
ISBN: 978-1-4620-6020-7 (ebk)

Printed in the United States of America

iUniverse rev. date: 10/24/2011

CONTENTS

PREFACE

Though there are thousands of pet care books out on the market today, but few address the growing concerns to cease treating our companion animals as mere property and to finally give them the companion status they deserve. With this in mind, we must become their guardians—not owners—and begin to give them more liberal and positive treatment and care. This book moves us forward to an evolving guardianship in which our companion animals are treated with both dignity and humanity. This publication will give you tools to journey toward this goal even as we move through the twenty-first century and beyond. Until we begin to consider our companion animals as part of an extension of our families, we will continue to lose the battle of raising the level of care to a more respectable status. Humans have genetically engineered and designed the companion animal to a degree that they are grossly dependent upon human protection. Therefore, we are charged with the responsibility to upgrade our companions' treatment and care if we want to see them live prosperous, healthy lives. Good luck and hug your companions daily!

Acknowledgments

I have been enriched with wonderful resources that have taught me to be a better parent to my extended family of four-legged companions and a humanitarian to all my animal friends: domestic, farm, and wild. If it weren't for those wonderful rescuers, animal rights advocates, activists, liberators, and friends, I would not be able to provide the public with resources for more humane tactics in caring for our beloved companion animals.

Many thanks go to my brother, Rocco Nunley, for his assistance with the funds needed to publish my second book. Thanks to Robert Denney, my colleague and friend, for his encouragement and support and for providing me with the outstanding cover illustration for my second publication . . . dweeb!

ILLUSTRATIONS AND REFERENCES

Illustrations:

Illustrations within this book are provided by both the author and her trusted comrade, Robert Denney, who donated photos of some of his four-legged family members in support of this book; Pongo (front cover) and Kleine (Pomeranian), who lost her sight a year back, are illustrated in chapter two. Kibbles the Shih-Tzu is my Aunt Sarah's baby. My spoiled crew includes Abigale, Kadie, Suzie Q, Lucy-Lu, and the "big-head," Vincent D'Puprio!

References:

Some commentaries and recommendations are also influenced and/or referenced by the following local and national animal welfare organizations, activist groups, local veterinarians, professionals, and advocates:

Supporters, members, and associates of ARM (Animal Rights Mercenaries, http://www.animalrightsmercenaries.com)

Wooftips.com

The US Department of Agriculture. *Federal Register Statement* 1996 (July 2, 1996).

Journal of the American Veterinary Medical Association (September 15, 2000), *JAVMA, Vol 217, No. 6, September 15, 2000 pg 836*

American Kennel Club (AKC)

The Humane Society for the United States (HSUS)
PawsHumane—Columbus

American Society for the Prevention of Cruelty to Animals (ASPCA)

People for the Ethical Treatment of Animals (PETA)

NOTATIONS

Throughout this book, I will not use the word "pets" or "property" in a positive light. All domestic animals will be referred to as companions or with other, friendlier terms. The word "owner" also will be represented in several instances in this book in a negative connotation. Positive words, such as "guardians" or "friends," will be used when referring to prospective and current animal lovers. Other positive terminologies will be used throughout this publication. As an activist, I also do not support the use of "it" or "property" where our companion animals are concerned.

If you would like additional information or to submit any comments, suggestions, or feedback related to this publication, you may contact the publisher through the following:

anticrueltycampain@yahoo.com

INTRODUCTION

Abigale   Kadie   Suzie   Lucy-Lu   Vincent O'Puprio

I sleepily turn my head and see Kadie (mixed terrier and Pug) snoring and snuggling right up against my head every time I stir. Then her panting and dog breath greet me immediately upon opening my eyes as she wags her tail in excitement and anticipation. Trying hard not to get up for fear of losing my spot, I see the others stretched out between the two beds in my room. Vincent, the Dane, has acquired the majority of my bed, leaving the three others (Suzie, Lucy and Abigale) plenty of space on the bed next to mine. The minute I decide to get up, I truly think there is a competition as to who is going to steal Mom's spot when I come back from a quick bladder break. I must, yet again, use some conning to get them to move so I can perform my ritualistic race with them back to the bed to get a prime spot before they get it.

Throughout the night, they will nudge their way as close as possible to me, forcing me into a tiny and almost insufficient space on the bed where I have to settle for the rest of my slumber. This routine is a daily occurrence, day or night, and I have been accustomed to their antics for several years. What parent doesn't go through humorous routines for their loved ones—dog or human child? You must have commitment, unconditional love, and loyalty when deciding on the leap into canine adoption.

Adopting or rescuing a companion animal is an immense responsibility and should never be taken lightly. As a potential parent/guardian, you will be the sole provider for that pure or mixed breed who depends on your love and protection throughout the rest of his or her life. It will prove to be the most profound and rewarding experience you will ever embark upon once you choose this unselfish path to help a companion animal receive the quality of life he or she so richly deserves. As humans constantly evolve and find better ways to improve their own lives, it is equally important to weigh in on the importance of advancing our best friends' care. Humans must come to the realization that domestic companions live each day dependent on us to survive.

Man, throughout time, has genetically engineered the domesticated animal. In return, it is our inherent responsibility to treat them with humanity, dignity, and loyalty in return. They impart unconditional love upon us every moment of their existence. I have compiled a few of the many articles I've written in the past to guide you to more liberal and positive directions in regard to companion animals' treatment and care. In this forum, I will primarily discuss the basics in the decision-making process in regard to adoption, responsible canine care, and some helpful tips that will sustain your companion care throughout your companion's lifetime.

You may find that many of these ideas can be slightly modified and incorporated into the humane care and maintenance of more than just our canine friends. Some suggestions can reach out to the many different species within the domestic animal umbrella. Let's upgrade our canine care and bring everyone into the twenty-first century and beyond in regard to sharing our lives with our beloved canines.

As a veteran consultant and guardian within Georgia, I have spent years in private fostering and adoptions around various counties within Midwest Georgia and east-central Alabama. I've published articles and tips via the Internet, local bulletin boards, electronic bulletins, and some of our local media, reaching out across the public safety divisions and general population within the surrounding counties in Midwest Georgia.

I have managed adoptions, rescue, and re-homing of homeless companion animals for almost a decade, including felines. I have donated personal funds (in excess of $10K) in spaying, neutering, and veterinary care for every animal I directly rescued before re-homing them to local families since 2002. I have been an advisor on canine-related issues within the public safety arena and families as well as to citizens across Muscogee County and its surrounding counties since my retirement from the military.

As an advocate and activist, some of our local venues have sought interviews and advice from me in reference to animal-related issues, including pit bull treatment, anti-chaining, canine attacks, and spaying and neutering. I've assisted the outlying areas with repairs and the construction of proper containment and housing for dogs in need of shelter, assisting both the citizens and their companions. I assist in donations and distribution of food, doghouses, crates, and equipment to local citizens throughout the year.

I am a supporting member to many groups, including the ASPCA, PAWsHumane Columbus, and HSUS. My benchmark organization, Wooftips.com, has donated funds in support of AngelDogRescue-GA and K-9 Hospice-AR for several years. After the restructuring and reorganization of my group, I founded my new organization, AnimalRightsMercenaries.com, to promote total animal liberation for domestic, farm, and wildlife, and contribute monthly to several local and national groups. Though I primarily offer private consulting, I have participated in community events, such as the annual Relay for Dogs sponsored by the American Cancer Society. My focus includes home safety and security, anti-cruelty campaigning, anti-chaining, and the banning of long-term crating, dog fighting issues, and spaying and neutering promotions.

You should always seek further advice from your local veterinarian related to any medical issues or concerns. They are a good point of reference when it comes to animal health and wellbeing. This book is a compilation of articles I put together throughout my years of working with companion animals, advocating and teaching others about animal rights through private and public consultations and Internet media.

Though the novice guardian will embark upon new territory, he or she will find the experience truly rewarding. Veteran guardians may also learn a humane tip or two from some of these helpful articles. Let's move forward with some basic tips for you to apply throughout your future coexistence with our domestic companions.

Chapter 1

Are You Ready for the Commitment?
Human versus Dog

Let's first gear our discussion toward when it is a good time to adopt a dog and the physical and social considerations that go into that huge undertaking. I may not have answers for every species of animal in regard to animal welfare. However, since I have been working with our canine friends for several years in the advocacy, parenting, consulting, and rescue capacities, I may be able to give you some insight as to what you need to know when you make that life-altering move toward bringing a loyal canine companion into your home and life.

As an advocate for animal rights, it may seem that I am scaring you away from adoption in the first few chapters. In fact, I am attempting to show you, as the prospective parent, a true picture of what it will be like to adopt a canine into your home. Trust me, when you are ready to adopt, you will find all these considerations are worth all the effort. It is both a reward and a privilege for a human being to discover the unconditional love a dog will bring into his or her life.

Before you take on the commission as a parent to a newfound canine companion, please take a look at yourself carefully and weigh your individual lifestyle considerations, environmental factors, and financial obligations. You need to make a very honest and upfront self-evaluation of your own character. In other words, don't ever just think of you—think of this non-human animal. When you take on this new life, you will have teamed up with this loyal animal companion and friend for the rest of your life!

What is your first impression when you think of living your life with a canine companion? Some think of them as a loyal companion going on walks in the park or tossing the Frisbee or ball in the countryside. Possibly you see yourself lounging on your couch, cuddling next to your furry friend while watching your favorite show. Others perceive dogs as partners in competitive events or shows. Perhaps you see a dog's additional charge as your guardian and protector of the family. Just make sure your dog is not some temporary replacement friend or fad for your five-year-old that shouts out "I want a puppy!"

Serious guardians look at a dog as a devoted companion that they will share their lives with—just as they would a child—not as a separate entity. All companion animals require routine vaccinations and checkups—and there is always the possibility that illness or injury will require medical expenses on top of routine shots and preventative meds. They will need shelter, proper nutrition, and fresh water at all times and some positive re-enforcement training throughout their lives.

There are obvious things to consider when you "opt to adopt," which I will discuss, but remember they are not just a physical responsibility you take on, but a social and mental responsibility as well. Dogs are living, breathing creatures that mankind has been entrusted to protect to ensure their sustainability and livelihood. They need play, exercise, and grooming, as one would logically consider. And they are not an "it" and should never be treated as property. Some things that you may not be aware of are the daily companionship, times of forgiveness, and your unselfish commitment through the trials and tribulations of both your lives.

It's not an option anymore to go on a vacation or trip upstate or abroad without considering your animal companion! You may find that your family needs will suddenly and without warning change in the future—relocations, downsizing, expansions, or births—and your faithful companion must also be part of your life-changing plans. He or she is supposed to be your lifelong companion, not a temporary resident. Many guardians falsely claim their dogs are their best friends. They will be quick to drop them the moment they encounter challenges, but if you look at it, their loyal companion animal may have been there well before these problems existed. There can be unforeseen instances, but guardians should always take their animals into consideration when moving or increasing the human size of their families. We need to remember that dogs love interaction and fellowship.

Activists, rescue organizations, welfare groups, and I would love it if every shelter dog (or any domestic companion animal) on the planet could be adopted into a loving family; however, we all know that it takes a special character of humans to be ready for the responsibilities of caring for a companion animal. Each animal has specific needs. Canines come with unique needs as does a ferret or a macaw. Whether you believe humans should or should not have engineered the domesticated breeds, we are all tasked with responsibilities now.

Some may not have the means or the right environment to adopt a dog; they would be far more suitable in other animal welfare-related capacities. Though a person's environment or status may not be right for the more direct adoption route, he or she may opt to assist a local shelter or national organization on the financial or fostering level. Programs exist to help construct containments/fencing to free a dog from a dismal life of tethering. Perhaps you may look into volunteering alongside groups that assist in building shelters for the defenseless animals left out in the harsh elements. You have so many more options than just picking up a dog from the shelter because you felt sorry for him or her. If you are still settled and ready in your mind to adopt, perhaps your choice will be about the type or breed of animal you adopt. You may be more suited to a different species in need, such as adopting a rescued cat, bird, rodent, or reptile. Whatever your choice on animal adoption or level of involvement, be sure that your decision is based on long-term commitment and the desire to impact that creature in a positive way—not the mere need for a feel-good change that may be just a passing fancy.

Additionally, the entire network of family around you must be equally involved in that decision process. Whether you are single, have a small or large family, are an apartment dweller, or reside with a significant other or roommate, everyone should be equally involved in your decision. Will they be a positive or negative influence in your adoption choice? Just because you love animals, that does not always mean you live in a perfect environment to adopt—at least for the time being. This should open your eyes to looking into the many available alternatives for you to positively contribute to our animal friends in need. Since not everyone is cut out for these types of responsibilities, weigh them carefully. Don't allow self-serving vanity to override the welfare of an animal companion. Following your heart and doing your research will help you make the right choices at the right time. Remember that all parties must be involved in order to give your new domestic companion a chance for a great life.

CHAPTER 2

Shelters or Stores: Let Your Conscience Be Your Guide

Let's get our paws into what is involved in the decision to adopt. The next thing I need to talk about is a subject no one wants to touch due to its sensitivity. We must decide whether to choose between adoptions through rescue agencies or buying an animal companion from a local pet store or breeder. Activists and welfare advocates would like you to consider the adoption route first.

Before you consider purchasing a companion, at least consider these hard-to-swallow truths. Puppy mills are one of the primary sources that retailers use in the accumulation and marketing of animals. If we continue to support these unregulated chains, these business-minded people will breed more and more puppies that could face an uncertain future. Is the animal's welfare truly considered in this equation? Pop-up breeders may not have the animal's welfare in mind and may be purely interested in their personal financial goals. Many businesses and breeders are not reputable and regard our companions as a marketable commodity or mere property. The bottom line is that the general public has little idea of the abuse, neglect, over-breeding, and unhealthy living environments that a dog comes from when they decide on the purchasing route.

Dogs, like every domestic, farm, or wild animal have long been considered man's property, which they may farm, collect, breed, test, and disseminate to their selfish and financial whims. It has been proven time and again that these establishments have been investigated and taken down due to their gross inhumanities. Many of these profit-minded institutions having little or no regulations in place to control their management. Due to breeder and/or retail chain irresponsibility, the communities are left to absorb the millions of malnourished, neglected, and abused dogs that will be looking to be placed into one of the many over-extended shelter facilities. Every dog you purchase from these unregulated establishments will increase the demand, thus taking another shelter dog out of the equation of a human's adoption consideration. This is bringing us further and further away from resolving the overpopulation problems we already face on a daily basis.

The more you buy from "pet" stores, the more dogs will have to be bred to replace them. Television commercials reference the overpopulation problems we face nationwide. Shelters have become overcrowded and funds are constantly whittled away from them every time humans opt to purchase a living creature. Until the mindset changes and we educate citizens about spaying and neutering, we will continue to see hundreds of homeless and abandoned living creatures in our neighborhoods. Until we consider them important additions to our family structures—rather than labeling them as commodities—we will continue to watch abuse rise and overpopulation remain in existence.

Many argue that the pedigree and/or breeder route is the way to go. Pedigree should be synonymous to human vanity. A dog could care less if he or she has a pedigree. It is only the parent (guardian) who chooses this rationale to serve personal preferences. Have you considered that many of these pedigree breeds are in fact in a shelter somewhere? I argue this point. Let's say you buy a Shar Pei from a breeder with a long line of pedigrees for $3,500. I would almost bet my paycheck that you could find that exact breed somewhere in a shelter or private no-kill establishment within a state or two, travel there, spend the adoption fees, spaying and/or neutering fees, shots, and the trip back at a fraction of what it would cost if you went the other route. Countless shelters are inundated with abandoned, abused, homeless purebreds that found unfortunate situations and are waiting for someone to bring them into a new and loving home.

Do your research! Due to legal stipulations, shelters cannot advertise a dog they rescue as purebred unless papers just happened to be attached to the dog's collars when they rescue the poor fellah. Soldiers deploying or even civilians undergoing sudden setbacks will many times drop little Oscar off at the local shelter or pound in hopes that someone will come along and save them from certain euthanasia. Some very good "pet" stores have shelters come out each weekend to their premises, affording the public an opportunity to adopt a homeless companion. These establishments allow guardians the option to adopt, forgoing the purchasing route. They volunteered to assist their local animal humane societies to help shelter animals get a second chance. Additionally, there are always neighbors that took on too many dogs or who didn't responsibly spay or neuter their animals who may have a little guy that needs a home before being hauled off to the local pound. The litter may have been accidental. I will give you that. Regardless of what locale you gained your newfound friend from, you should always have them immediately spayed and/or neutered. Stress to your neighbors to have their companions spayed and neutered . . . please!

Some reputable organizations put on huge events to support local humane societies and agencies in service to our shelter animals.

Many provide thousands upon thousands of dollars into non-profit programs that survive almost entirely because of their generosity. It is fair to say that some of these large events have some positive impact. I will ask you to first consider the adoption route in order to help millions of homeless animals get off the street and find a solid family network. If all we do is continue to breed show and vanity dogs while numbers constantly increase inside the shelters, we are actually burning the candle on both ends. I wonder if the scales are in fact tipping. It's a fact that more dogs are being born each day from breeders continuously looking to find that "best in show" dog while the remaining litter faces a questionable future, impacting the overall population increase of dogs. The figures must be overwhelming so I always encourage adopting from a local rescue organizations as a first choice. Consider compromising and adopt one of your new companions from the local shelter.

Be a considerate and caring human savior and adopt a homeless dog who only desires to please and give unconditional love to someone. In my small city, it is broadcasted daily on the radio that more than 8,000 animals were rescued and taken into the city's Animal Resource Center yearly (as of 2010 according to PawsHumane-Columbus)—and almost 7,000 end up euthanized. This is an example of a sad yet constant truth within many animal control centers across the nation. Fortunately, there have been great strides in moving toward adopting "no kill" policies throughout shelters nationwide including our own hometown (2011). This is one of the many positive initiatives going on throughout the nation which were greatly influenced by caring city leaders, citizens and local activists' efforts alike. An additional way for future guardians of our animal friends to help reduce these numbers is to choose to adopt a rescue from a local shelter. Don't forget that an equally implied task here is to spay or neuter! I can't stress that enough! Yes, I went into soapbox mode there for a moment to quickly convince you to choose adoption over retail. Please take additional time to read up on this important issue via your libraries, bookstores, and internet to familiarize yourself with the advantages. Take a moment to stop by a local animal welfare organization and get their expert opinions on the subject.

CHAPTER 3

Breed and Need: General Insight

Let's look briefly into the breed choice in respect to your needs. Since we are targeting the canine bunch, you should consider what breed type will be appropriate for your lifestyle and environment. Since there are countless publications on this subject matter, I will only highlight a few criteria by experience. Consider animal size, exercise level of you and the dog, physical dwellings, personality traits, other family members' preferences within the household, and purpose. I will generalize the person's lifestyle with short comparison to a dog and then we will go into the breeds and their distinctive temperaments.

In my household, I may have more of a preference to short-haired dogs. I could care less if they are short or tall, mixed or pure, as long as there is one less shelter or abandoned dog. Others may have unique needs that make them just as responsible, but they opt for a dog that works well with their lifestyle. Active individuals may want to partner up with a terrier in their quest to jointly find pleasure in agility competitions. Perhaps "walker" or "river rats" may find refuge in adopting a retriever or hound. I won't entertain the hunter since this would go against my humanitarian views. However, you can find information about that issue in other forums—as many know, it is a large commercial sport. More mature empty-nesters may opt for the quick and alert working dog who likes to be territorial and protective over his mom and/or pop and alert when others may be at the door. Who can forget the guardians that love to primp and fuss over their smart companion to forever dote over? They may be more predisposed toward the cute toy or a statelier breed. Some love a feeling of satisfaction. It would be also safe to assume those dogs love all that fuss and muss if they are handled properly—spoiled, I should say! Some breeds are docile and perfect "one dog" companions for certain individuals.

Perhaps you are a young, energetic entrepreneur, working at home who is strong natured and desires to rescue a Dane or Mastiff or Doberman in a local rescue organization that has hundreds of these particular rescues on the premises. Though large, they don't require as much room as one may assume. Don't rule out big guys and opt only for the tiny guys. I have an entire chapter discussing this issue on the comparisons of the two groups. Depending on mobility and strength, many small and large breeds have similar characteristics but differ in size. Be aware that very large breeds of dogs may be more prone to shorter life expectancy than smaller breeds. Some dogs that have thick or second coats may actually shed less than others. A schnauzer will shed less than perhaps a short haired Labrador. Apartment dwellers should consider the "yappiness" and proximity to neighbors and the need for outside playtime.

A dog is a very good way to assist in your exercise regiments. A companion canine almost forces you to become more active should you want to become sedentary a bit too early in your life. Dogs are great therapy dogs for the elderly, children, and that harbor unique medical conditions and challenges. I have a child with mental and physical challenges that help entertain and stimulate her development. Many professionals in the area of animal behavior will stipulate that dogs help extend people's lives and improve their personality. I can't speak for the experts, but I've seen the grumpiest of the lot become more caring and loving when parenting a canine. Once you've allowed a frisky or loving canine behind that lonely cage in the shelter to find you, you will understand the depth of loyalty and love a dog can give someone—freely and without coercion!

Consider the mixed breed in the thousands of shelters. Though you may be a staunch Beagle lover, you may find that Lab, Rottweiler, hound (whatever mix) that is lonely in the shelter has caught your attention. With his love and affection that he will show the rest of his living days, he may end up the best dog you've ever partnered up with. Many folks—even some celebrities—boast how their mixed guys have given them unlimited happiness and love! Perhaps a Chihuahua may be too delicate for you, but when it is mixed with a tenacious terrier or dachshund or some other crazy fellah, he or she may turn out to be the incredible super dog with plenty of durability and sustainability. One never knows.

The best recommendation I can give folks that are choosing a future furry companion is to go to the local animal shelter and just walk. When the time and opportunity is right, there will some magnetic attraction between you and your future companion behind that wire cage. Understand the price you pay in pet stores will be more than the cost if you do your homework and find the little/big guy in a rescue facility. It's a fact that most dogs will pick their family! Just give them a chance when the time is right for you.

CHAPTER 4

Group Temperament and Impact on Healthy Coexistence

We can break down the groups and the temperament. The amusing thing is how professionals and the everyday layperson describe the temperament of a breed. Since there are really as many variations to defining words as there are dogs when it comes to characterizing a specific breed, everything becomes subjective through the eyes of the observer. Most experts will agree that all dogs—purebred or not—have unique characteristics in behavior from various factors to include their upbringing, socialization, and genetic background. The guardian's characteristics will have some impact on the companion's behavior as well. Since this is true, it will pose a bit of a challenge to give you some insight as to breed behavior and temperament. I will try to break it down as close to what I see on a routine basis.

Though many will give you the scientifically accepted opinion, they have concluded their findings through observation. It would stand to reason that we—simple guardians that spend massive amounts of interaction around our favorite domestic companions—can do the same. We can agree to disagree when it comes to every dog having unique social behaviors and whether they were engineered by man. However, no matter the DNA and manipulation of genes, guardians have some influence in how they developed—just like human beings. Since we are all mammals, it could be inferred that humans and dogs gain their personalities as they go through life. Nevertheless, we have to acknowledge their genetic makeup has a considerable influence on their overall temperament.

Organizations and experts in canine sociology agree that each group possesses a wide range of temperaments. I've been privileged to grow up around many of these breed categories and I have firsthand knowledge that some of these professionals are right on target with their assessments. We activists can be happy to give them their just credit.

Groups of dogs are typically broken down by the large labeled organizations, such as the American Kennel Club: Sporting, Non-sporting, Hound, Terrier, Toy, Working, Herding, and Miscellaneous Breeds. Other countries modify the groups to their interpretations. England's sporting group is labeled the Gundog Group. Groupings are fluid and change according to breed characteristics, but they are pretty set on those eight categories in the twenty-first century.

My group of mixed breed terrors would fall under the miscellaneous group, but I suppose the AKC would be quick to notice they have no pedigree. Regardless, our garden-variety guardians may want a basic level of description and character of our companion animals to give them a start as to what to look for in adoption.

In general, the Sporting, Hounds, Working, Terriers, Toy, and Miscellaneous groups are basically what I will go with. Some time ago, dogs were primarily bred for a general purpose and the working, sport, and hunting classes were prevalent in the world of canine show. Though the hounds have the prime task as the hunters—much as those characterized in the sporting group—they were separated because of their unique characteristics. Additionally, the hounds represent quite a large group to be mixed with the sport. The toy group perhaps evolved from pure desires to have dogs as cuddling companions. I look at all of them as my children sharing my couch and being lifelong buddies. Miscellaneous groups are in a sort of limbo state; they are versatile and may end up going into the other groups after time. No matter the breed group, all dogs are understandably high rated and equally important!

We have a broad spectrum of breed categories and all of them are growing and evolving. I can't even keep up with the standard to put the many dogs we have in our country. Breeds are developing and coming into the many registries every year. Usually after some panel decides they have had enough lineage, developmental years, and distinct purpose, they will be chosen to acquire national recognition and status. Regardless of their status and worth designated by the many professionals, dog lovers could care less about status and vanity rankings.

Now all we have to do is put some kind of opinion together to assess these guys in relation to temperament. I caution you to never base your decision about a dog group from a bad experience or someone who may have had just one incident. This isn't enough time or reason to make a comprehensive evaluation. You must understand that people who have dug down and evaluated every single breed have spent many years of scientific study to evaluate them.

The AKC is a wonderful resource to get an idea of a particular breed. However, I try to emphasize that some people will have the opposite experience to what experts in that field may have encountered with a particular breed. I will focus on the overall group and give some generalized observations to assist in making an informed decision.

Consider the general temperament of the group and then you can decide on the size and breed choice, weight ranges, and coats in regard to your own particular likes. I will do the best I can to give you an indiscriminate impression of the lot. Others may reference through complex graphs or technical scientific analysis, but I'm going to just approach this from a layperson's perspective. Like humans, nature and/or nurture can always modify each mammal's behavior so everything is subjective.

The Hounds: This is a considerably large group that encompasses a great number of breeds. If you saw these guys, you would think they need a separate show just to present this fine crew to the public. These guys are designed for tracking and/or hunting down something by primarily scent and sight. These dogs range from a simple twelve-pound Whippet to a large 130-pound Irish Wolf-Hound. Hounds were noticeably bred through the years with the size and stature to adapt to the ground level in which they would be working. Hounds are also characterized as sight or scent hounds and the particular breed will highlight those characteristics. Some have extraordinary ears low to the ground with large drooping snouts to sniff out their objectives while sight hounds will be quick, agile, long, and lean. All are designed and engineered to better accomplish the mission at hand.

If you want a laudable and inquisitive dog, these guys are for you. These guys work well (if raised together) in packs and as individuals. Their temperament can be quite diverse—although in typical scenarios, they tend to be consistent with their behaviors. Thus guardians that decide on these dogs must have quite a bit of patience if they are attempting to re-channel them in other directions. Don't get a hound and expect them not to want plenty of room and time outdoors to dig, climb, explore, and forage. They can be relentless in their quests and you will rarely see them halting their activities until they tire themselves out. Give these dogs plenty of space to run around or track down a vermin as their instincts call for. They are usually better in country settings. They tend to be stubborn and need plenty of reinforcement. Smaller ones can be quite guardian-intensive and territorial. They are consistent breeds throughout their adulthood, but guardians rarely observe them becoming aggressive in a pushy manner. However, the smaller ones may have serious Napoleon complexes just as some of the toy groups maintain. Indoors, these guys can be pretty laid back—but once you get them outside, I suggest you keep an eye on them. Have very good fencing and containment and definitely spay or neuter them. They will seek or sniff out the opposite sex quite a distance away. Though they do harbor consistent behaviors, depending on whether they are obsessive or not, you may find it difficult to change their ways. A tree hound wants to always be a tree hound and those bloodhounds as do their Beagle buddies stay consistent with their diligence to search out and explore. Whether they are 100 percent accurate (must have some training to master specific tasks), they look for whatever will spark their interests.

Most of these dogs are not quiet. They range from the howling big ones to the yappy smaller ones. These guys aren't just barking at someone. It is almost a form of entertainment and socialization for them; perhaps they just like the sound of their bark. Aside from the occasional noise, the majority are absolutely durable and well-rounded dogs. Most hound guardians know the neighbors may become annoyed if they are not used to these guys. Usually, their tones are on a lower decibel—and not the overbearing high-pitched barking you may be accustomed to. Some neighbors will tolerate their barking better than some of the other group barkers. Typically, the hound groups are found on larger plots of country land or in the outskirts of the city. Though the hounds are very lovable, they tend to give their attention to you when they feel like it. Usually, they are the most catlike of the bunch. They love you to be around but they aren't always snugglers.

I would place Dachshunds, however, in their own special category since one will never know what they are thinking. Those guys are quite the comical crew and still possess the stubbornness one must adapt to. It's all in a matter of how much or little training the hound group gets. They instinctively love being out and about scoping the property and coming in and out at their leisure.

They do seem to be startled quickly, especially the sight groups of these hounds. Their alertness is quite prominent in almost all of them. I watched a local hunt club that had hundreds of hounds and I saw some of their similarities. It was interesting to see the new ones trained to track and go on large events. Of course, I am the last one to go track down an animal. However, you must recognize that it is an inherited trait for these breeds to track. Luckily this particular organization holds their events as purely recreational and allows no animals to be harmed. Those individuals or groups who use weapons around hounds typically train the dogs around them.

Since sight hounds will react to sudden movements and sounds, hunters teach them early on to adapt to gunfire. For the rest of the non-hunters, we know that these guys are very keen to noises and we need to comfort and console them.

"Ground pounders" as I like to refer them to, such as Bassets and Bloodhounds are constantly honed in on what they are looking for, but they still need their instincts reinforced from time to time. The heavier the breed, the more likely their activity levels will be limited. Plenty of rest between activities is encouraged to avoid physical trauma. These aren't the typical play-around dogs for younger children, but they will accommodate them sporadically. Their idea of playing may differ than other breeds. I wouldn't categorize them as fetchers in most cases so they may not fulfill the typical kid mentality. Being raised around children is usually the best for these guys and then they are great with them. Otherwise they can become temperamental and lack the patience to handle the younger-minded population. Usually these are mature guys' dogs or folks who do like to go out on leisurely hikes or outside trekking.

The Sporting Group: Those dogs whose primary mission is sport encompass the sporting group. They participate and are instinctively designed with a sense of hunting just as the hounds are. The difference lies in the characteristics. The basic difference between hounds and sporting group dogs is that the sporting group consists of all the other hunting dogs not in the hound category. Hounds are all "hound breeds" and the sporting groups have hundreds of classified breeds within their dominion. Though hunting may not be my interest, I will say this group is bred specifically for this type activity in mind. The most common breeds you will see in this category are dogs, such as Retrievers, Spaniels, and Setters.

These guys typically need a bunch of exercise and to be kept occupied. I've had the opportunity to have lived with—and fostered—more breeds in this category than of any other group. If you don't give these guys something constructive to do, they tend to find something to do on their own and become destructive. Not giving them an activity or exercise will cause these breeds to become overweight later in their lives. Since the retrievers are common to this group, guardians that have cared for these dogs know they are quite active to midlife and can become obese quickly. They tend to do well with other dogs; since they are not as territorial as many of the other breeds, hunters and sports enthusiasts love to bring these guys to outdoor events.

Socially, they have been highly adaptable and have been a favorite for the young and old. Their behavior seems to remain constant throughout their lives—barring any abuse or neglect—and they are more versatile perhaps than any other breed. I know from experience that these breeds are notorious shedders and can get quite dirty due to their instinctive curiosity and need to explore the outdoors. Most guardians will find they are not ridiculously territorial and are quite tolerant to unfamiliar people.

Depending on their training, a dog in this category can have any of these character traits. Most of the breeds within the sporting group are submissive, friendly, eager to please, and adaptable. Overall, I would say these dogs are favored within several communities as family companions that can please sports enthusiasts and active families that enjoy outings, camping, and water sports.

The Working Group: These guys are classified as the dogs that guard, rescue, herd, or guide. These dogs are not usually the small breeds. In fact, if someone would go to a typical dog show, they would see some rather well-defined, muscular, stout dogs in this group. German Shepherds, Malamutes, Sheepdogs, Huskies, St. Bernard's, Dobermans, Great Danes, and Burmese Mountain Dogs are a few. These fellahs have been bred for a specific purpose with working humans. They are many times trained to be involved in specialized conditions and missions. They are commonly found within medical professions as therapy dogs, search and rescue, or protection services. This group ranges from the stubborn though docile Great Danes to the consistent and trainable German Shepherds and Belgian Malinois.

These dogs range in mentality according to their training. Left untrained, these dogs will be unpredictable and will adapt to their surroundings. These dogs are routinely acquired by those who love both stately, intimidating dogs. Folks that like a dog that possesses a strong will and good character consider them the dogs of choice. These are multipurpose dogs that come with multifaceted personalities. Families, young professionals, and laborers love these dogs. They are usually very good around families. They are trained young in this capacity and possess average to above average intelligence.

Dobermans, Rottweilers, Burmese Mountain Dogs, and Mastiffs have lovable personalities if raised in this manner. Many believe these dogs are even re-trainable after some unfortunate encounters with abuse—depending on the extent—but you may be wary of their history and background. Most of the time, these breeds get a bad rap; the impression they are highly dangerous and will eat you the minute you come on the premises, but most of the larger breeds within this group are quite the opposite and only defend when they perceive a threat. These dogs can seem scary.

The shepherds (herders) can range from dominant to submissive, depending on how they are treated. Guardians with these breeds will usually tell you they are quite protective of them the more attention they get. Herding dogs are also known for their high intelligence.

Since Danes, Mastiffs, St. Bernards, and other huge breeds within this category seem to stand out, you must not direct all your attention to them if you have other dogs. With my Great Dane, I must be cautious to not always give him all the attention because he will naturally become overly territorial and clingy. I found this can be also true with the various Rottweilers, Dobermans, and Boxers I've been fortunate enough to have cared for during the past twenty years.

I have studied this breed of dog in more depth within the last decade. I've seen and interacted with enough of these dogs to know it would be well to understand and respect these fellahs! Most of their temperament is constant, but it usually doesn't show until they are out of those mischievous puppy stages. Dogs within this group are somewhat of a handful for newbies that aren't familiar with the working group mentalities. They will announce themselves and tear up your house, causing a train wreck very quickly if you don't give them positive training and meaningful activities. Older dogs will become sedentary. However, they will still possess those territorial traits.

Dogs in this category are quite unstable when over-bred. German shepherds and Rottweilers were publicized for some time as frequently over-bred and inbred by irresponsible breeders. People who were not aware of these problems would either get rid of them or abuse them just as quickly as they brought them in. Thus some of these breeds suffered a lot of bad press due to instabilities in certain regions. Anyone getting one of these should read up on them extensively and gather as much history on the breed choice as possible. Additionally, these dogs do considerably well in solitary situations whereas some other groups love to have a pack around them. If you want a territorial breed, you will definitely find these traits in most of the working class. Throughout my travels and experience in the South, folks either love or hate this breed.

The Terrier Group: I personally label these guys the tenacious terrors of the dog groups. These guys pack energy beyond belief and usually are hearty, compact, and durable. These dogs can range from Cairns, Fox Terriers, Dandie Dinmonts, Airdales, Irish, Lakelands, and Bedlingtons to the American Staffordshire and Bull Terriers. Since these dogs, no matter the size, won't back down to even the largest of contenders, people have unfortunately used our companions of this group for bull baiting, dog fighting, and other cruel sports. The smaller breeds are common in several agility competitions due to their tenacity and relentless endurance. Large segments of this group are highly abused in the animal world. The Staffordshire Pit Bull Terriers and other variations of the bull terriers have been popular in some areas within the US as pit dogs, fighting to their death while gawking, heartless spectators cheer them on. As repulsive as this is, it is highly prevalent in the South. I've seen countless arrests and reports of such accounts while working in the public safety arena. Many counties have pushed for Breed Specific Legislation

(BSL)—and many activists have become outraged since they know it is the handler who should be accountable, not the dog.

Terriers are what I describe as either active or very active in their demeanor, activity level, and personality. They are an extensive, well-rounded group inside or outside the household. These dogs don't care where they live as long as they can be active. If you keep them active, they are happy. If not, you commonly have a destructive monster on your hands. They range from the "zoomers" to the comical entertainers (i.e. the Jack Russells and Parsons) in this unique group. They do fair well with others, but many will tell you to raise them together. Otherwise they tend to get into mischief and be reserved in their abilities to accept others (dog or human) within their surroundings.

Though easy to train, their attention span is more like a person with moderate ADD. They are tenacious and persistent. They rarely back down until they are either killed or called off if they have received formal training. They are a vigorous bunch however; many will find the larger ones are basically gentler. The pedigree Staffordshire Bull Terrier is actually a dog with a wonderful temperament. Humans have toyed with their breeding and produced some unpredictable and unstable personalities. Free from abuse and raised properly, these dogs require moderate activity and are fantastic around children. Thousands of these variations of bull terriers are found in the South and guardians will be divided on their opinions of the breed.

Many organizations have popped up throughout the years to rescue and protect these widely abused dogs from one-track-mind owners. If you actually looked at them without subjecting them to abuse, you would see a group that is a well rounded and lovable. The terriers do go through some hellacious puppy times and guardians should be prepared for that. After that stage, they are not commonly known to tear up the household. They do love to dig so be quite aware of this! Parsons Fox Terriers are potential yard "zoomers and shakers" that have an active mind and physical stamina to match. They will go on for what seems like forever. They can be small or large.

Terriers range in their territoriality and for the most part are selfish. Guardians typically find strangers are not always welcomed by this group. The more you spoil these guys, the more they don't care for others and become standoffish. Experts agree if you submit to their behaviors and don't reinforce good training, they will become more dominant! Most of my friends have these breeds and I consistently see the same behaviors. This is also taking into account the fact that my friends are not the percentage of the populations that harm, fight, or neglect their terrier breeds. They are some of the favorite dogs of canine lovers and are well accepted throughout the country with proper guidance. These guys don't back off. They are notorious barkers, alerting you of some being's presence, challenge anyone regardless of size, and are usually protective of their territories. They can also dig up your yard and bring a tree into your house if you let them!

The Toy Group: Toy groups are specifically designed for those human "pooch huggers" that want a luxurious lap dog and cutesy companion to parade around their abode and neighboring sidewalks. These dogs support a human's vanity and codependence. These include Chihuahuas, Boston Terriers, Shih-Tzus, Pomeranians, Maltese, Papillons, Toy Poodles, and Manchesters. Many keep these dogs in a small apartment or upscale home. Not all small dogs, however, fall into the toy group—and some of the small guys fall into the other groups due to their industrious traits. For example, the dachshund is found in hound group and not the toy group. Standard Dachshunds are not as light as many may think. Some have bred them to the miniature sizes. Dogs that represent the toy group are usually extremely light and bred specifically with this in mind. Some experts put it in the average of eight to ten pounds. Without our care in all respects, these dogs will perish almost instantly! These dogs require a constant watchful eye—from threats of being swooped up by a hawk to shivering from the slightest temperatures or getting slammed in the car door. So many requirements are involved in caring for this group and I would be safe to say that they are not a durable dog. In fact, man has genetically altered the toy dog to such a small stature that I would argue they made them the most codependent group of all dogs on the planet.

This group was designed and engineered to accommodate the wealthy and high-maintenance public. These guys will get away with everything if you let them. Oh, but don't let their tiny size make you start feeling sorry for them because they will in fact, ruin your life! You got to love these guys though. If there is a spoiled group, this is the crew. On the other hand, this group can be easily abused primarily due to lack of education on the particular dog's needs! Some guardians initially spoil and dote over them. Then, they get tired of the responsibility and forget these little fellahs and just sweep them to the side like yesterday's fad. Too many times, folks don't realize that the toy group requires more maintenance and care than any other dog! They cannot fend for themselves from predators, uneducated and/or apathetic humans, or even rambunctious children. They think they are giants and super-dogs. They are not and cannot hold their own in almost any environmental circumstance. Their physical abilities are limited and they cannot survive harsh treatment—mentally or physically.

They love to please and are codependent. They require very little outdoor activity and tend to be quite active indoors. Space is of little issue when you adopt a dog from the toy group. However, allow them some different areas within your living space to satisfy their curious natures. Toy dogs may come off as submissive, but most guardians know they are the "con-dogs" of the lot! They are manipulative if you allow them to be. They range from the territorial and moody Chihuahuas all the way to the happy and lovable Pugs that will allow anyone to come in and join their party. They tend to learn very rapidly and are pretty good in the problem-solving capacity.

I've had the pleasure of living with breeds within this group alongside my large ones and I'm the first to tell you they can range from "My mom is gullible and I can woo her into anything" all the way to "I'm a Valley Girl, so whatever!" I've also fostered Chihuahuas that can absolutely run the household and scare off visitors faster than a large breed. I have had some that could care less who you are. Most of the toy group has come to like all the attention and almost demand it after they learn what they can and can't get away with. While the majority seem very bright, I have had seen some airheads—and living with them can be a challenge. We must love all personalities and look it as a special challenge, loving them just the same.

The absolute hardest challenge you will find with the toy group is the housetraining issue. I have found—along with many of my friends near and abroad—that toy breeds take much longer to housetrain than other breeds. As smart as these guys are, their perception of space is far different compared to larger dogs. Due to their size, they think they are a mile away when they pee in a room. They can be stubborn if you don't train them properly and will do things out of pure spite. They are quick learners, but some may take a time or two to sink in. The most important thing guardians should take away with toy breeds is that their size and physiological makeup constitutes an extremely codependent companion. You must protect them so they can live long lives. Little children must be introduced to breeds within this group with extra caution! These little guys are a hit with most everyone—the midlife folks, apartment dwellers, young couples, and the elderly.

The Miscellaneous Group: These are our guys that seem to fall into a category when they don't fall into the others. Though these guys may have abilities similar to a lot of those other guys, such as the retrievers or hounds, they were not intentionally bred into the specific breed or type as with the other groups. In fact, some of these dogs may be good at sport—or classified as a terrier or hound, for that matter—but someone opted to put them into this category for specific reasons. I could put hundreds of pooches in this category to include the typical Dalmatian, Lhasa Apso, poodles, and several varieties of bulldogs, some terriers, such as the Jack Russell Terrier, and even Vizlas. Some mixed varieties are placed into this grouping. If the experts can't decide on where to put a dog, they put it here in the miscellaneous group.

Again, we mentioned that these dogs by most rating categories don't really fall into the other groups. Though miscellaneous in grouping, they don't serve the same functionality as the others. Therefore, their characteristics and demeanor may vary from animal to animal. Many feel these guys are high learners, but others place them in the stubborn territorial category. Everything is subjective here since the dogs range from terrier to semi-work to the size of a toy dog. Even after much study, it's still unclear what criteria are involved. As cloudy as I am about their standards, I'm almost safe to say these are up and coming canines who will eventually find themselves in the other classes.

Regardless, some categorize dogs, such as the territorial and strong-willed Chow in this group. Even the adorable Bichon Frise fell into this group for some time. In fact, these miscellaneous dogs are quite popular perhaps because of their broad range of personalities. Whether a dog is a Dalmatian or Schipperke, the dogs within the miscellaneous group have a place in the canine lover's heart and home. There are thousands of things to consider when gaining a new family member in the house. We just don't have the time to delve into every one. I only touch briefly on a few categories of groups and breeds to describe some of the unique characteristics to consider. I will stress to you that the word "purpose" is quite broad in its interpretation and can be controversial. I'm only going to say that the primary purpose computed with all your self-direction should be that are going to be an extension of your family—so treat them as such! After this, you may opt to have additional reasons to have a new companion.

CHAPTER 5

Unconditional Love Brings Justifiable Costs

Few people consider the financial considerations that will be involved when adopting a newfound companion. As a parent and guardian to Romeo or Juliet, you must accept all that goes into caring for them in a loving and humane way. Here's a quick table (guideline only) to assist you on average costs that two medium-sized dogs may present in a year. We will use the medium-sized dogs (30-55 pounds) to give a broad picture and all. Additionally, I tend to encourage and emphasize to guardians to perhaps adopt a pair—teaming your dog up with another canine companion gives your pooch someone to play with when you are not around and helps to reduce some of their boredom. It gives them even more of a healthy life.

I will use costs in relation to a year. This will encompass adequate care—not cutting corners and not the absolutely cheapest route. I won't go the ridiculously expensive route since average citizens may never maintain such an endeavor. These are just basic care costs an average family will encounter when providing an adequate level of care to humanely exist. You can calculate up or down, according to the numbers and size as you see fit. I cannot predict emergencies or sudden trauma so these costs do not factor in sudden illnesses or accidents that may evolve. Just as having a child, there will be ups and downs to contend with should they get into those mischievous bouts. Four of my five are medium-sized dogs, but I've broke this down to an average household of two. A great number of my colleagues have two medium companions so I interviewed them as well and included average annual costs.

Here's the very basic breakdown with typical items to consider after you have already experienced the initial costs of bringing your companions: puppyhood, shelter, water bowls, beds, collars, leads, bedding, spaying and or neutering, microchips, first shots, and physicals, etc. This is merely the maintenance and upkeep for guardians wanting to give them a respectable quality of care. Everything can be relative according to location, economy, and contingencies. This is based on 2011 estimates:

Approximate cost calculated for year 2011. Prices are considered utilizing a typical animal retail chain in your areas (I'm using Georgia for example).			
Item	**Avg. Cost per item(s)**	**Annual cost**	**Remarks**
Food (Dry Food: did not factor in wet food for those who use this type)	$20-28 per 30 lb. bag	$240-$336	This would be regular consumption and a reputable healthy kibble. Always keep one contingency bag on hand to plan for a month of possible reduction in funds.
Treats	$6-$14 for 2 lbs.	$72-$168	Every guardian will consider treats for their adored companions.

Approximate cost calculated for year 2011. (Continued)			
Supplements and Vitamins	$26-$30 (365 count)	$52-$60	365 count on average bottle of vitamins so I am multiplying by two.
Flea and Tick Prevention	$20 per ampoule or oral pill per dog a month averaging 35-55 lbs.	$480	This has been my highest and typical cost for name brand flea, tick, and worm preventative. Don't skimp on these items, especially in the South! Many prefer holistic measures. Just keep in mind the cost will vary when going this route!
Heartworm Preventative	$6-$8 per dose per month	$72-$96	This is the name brand. Cheaper brands may not be as effective.
Veterinary Care (checkups and annual boosters)	$130-$300	$260-$600	This average includes city permits, rabies, annual boosters, and overall healthy dog checkup.

Approximate cost calculated for year 2011. (Continued)			
Boarding	$12-$20 per night	$120-$200 for ten visits in a year	This depends on how many days you have to board your dog in a year.
Grooming (typical bath, cut, nails, teeth, ears, undercoat, flea/tick baths and deodorizer	$45-$90 a basic package per dog	$540-$1,080	This is if you take both dogs every month. These totals can be greatly altered depending upon the services you opt for!
Dog Toys	$5-$15 per dog per month	$60-$180	This is considering wear and tear and replacements of just one toy per month! Most guardians will purchase a bit more than that.
Training		$100-$400	This is too broad of an area and depends on return reinforcement trainings or just a one package deal for six weeks sessions.

Approximate cost calculated for year 2011. (Continued)			
General Maintenance and Repairs	$30-$60	$360-$720	Dogs, like children, will inadvertently tear something up and/or cost you for various repairs, such as replacing screens, chewed up upholstery/furnishings. This is a common situation and guardians must account for these instances.
Totals		$2,250-$3,908	Minus training. This is from low average to high average on a typical year for both dogs
Totals		$2,359-$2,919	With training package. These are totals from low average to moderately high averages on a typical year with maintaining both dogs

CHAPTER 6

Top Five Reasons Not To Adopt

Animal lovers and activists want to see all homeless and abused companion animals in local shelters re-homed to a fine family. Unfortunately, some of these abandoned animals end up in the same situation they found themselves initially. Here are some of the most common mistakes of potential guardians. I am describing each situation in a bit of a satirical manner. These instances occur when folks go into the process without considering all the responsibilities that come with adding a new family member to their households.

One: "My son wants a puppy."

How many times do animal lovers and shelter agencies hear this phrase? Not every case in which a child wants a dog is bad idea. If you are totally prepared and it is a shared decision, then this would not be an issue. Unfortunately, the initial planning for this newfound friend is not in the parent's mindset. Kneejerk reactions can harm the dog. Many times dogs that are adopted without all the necessary research and planning are neglected, abused, abandoned, or returned to the facility they were originally adopted from. This is perhaps the number one reason why you shouldn't get a dog!

Inevitably, the young child that was fascinated by the little puppy ends up ignoring the dog. And, then the parent(s) get tired of feeding and caring for the dog since the child was the initial reason for getting a dog and they gave up caring for it. He or she has replaced Buster with various human playmates. Everyone knows that when a child wants a pup, that familiar phrase comes out of the parent's mouth: *You're going to have to feed and take care of the puppy, okay, Jimmy.* This is a complete fantasy! Children promise parents the moon at that moment and even parents think it's cool for Jimmy or Suzie to get a puppy, but in reality it should be the family's companion.

These adorable puppies will become dogs! A dog is perhaps ten times more likely to get abandoned, neglected, or re-homed because a child had a passing fancy for one. Get a dog for all the right reasons and for everyone concerned and not for a passing fad or flavor of the week.

Two: You don't have the basic necessities for you and/or your family's normal sustenance.

My neighbor hangs her family's clothes on the back fence of their corner house after washing them every week. She is always in a financial bind and has little time at home because of multiple low-paying, part-time jobs. Her yard is overgrown, and the house is in a horrible state of disrepair. So, which part of this equation is not a good time to have a dog? A four-legged companion is a lifelong responsibility, requiring routine veterinary care, nutritional needs, socialization, etc. Without this, the cute little puppy or dog you adopted ends up destroying your place out of boredom, malnourishment, mistreatment, or neglect. The majority of the time, the dog is placed outside and ignored for the remainder of its dismal existence. When you are physically, mentally, emotionally, and financially ready for a dog, then go ahead and adopt. Until then, plan and save up for later adoption or volunteer at a local shelter a few days per month. Maybe you are more suited to donate to a local organization if you want to help animals. Not everyone is suited for one reason or another to get a new companion—bird, cat, dog, or even a goldfish!

Three: The environment is not suited for a dog.

A family gets a goldfish. They get a nice large tank, food, and cute little things to entertain the guy at the bottom of the tank—maybe a few little caves and greenery to make it look like a little happy haven for the guy. Mom even faithfully cleans the tank once a week and might even get a couple of other little companions in the tank to keep him happy. The fish is a happy little camper with his friends and attention. Of course, you can maintain this little guy with very little effort.

However, (this is a true story too) what about a couple boasting about adopting a Labrador Retriever? The young couple is living in a small residence, working up to fifteen hours per day, with no fence, playground, or playtime. He sits inside a small kennel all day long till the family comes home. What kind of life is this for a dog? Families should think about the long-term and have healthy refuge set up before deciding on a dog.

First the fence, then the dog!

Even many so-called apartment dogs end up in kennels all day long while the family is gone and forget they have a faithful companion that has been patiently waiting for them. I say to people all the time, "No one forced you to adopt!" There is no set rule saying you have to have a dog. Have suitable accommodations for the particular size, breed, and type of domestic animal you plan on adopting. If this isn't planned out prior to adoption, the dog usually gets a new type of notice—a notice of an eviction and into the classifieds!

Four: The uneducated or misguided human brings in a dog.

The worst offenders are those who have been taught the *wrong* values in regard to their companion animals—many times through older family members, peers, and neighbors due to lack of education or worse. They view a living soul as mere property. The most common example in our region would be as follows: Little Jimmy's dad owns a dog for years, chained up in the back yard all the time and was utilized only as what his dad called a guard dog. Jimmy grows up thinking this is the way a dog should be treated—and that they are property and not a companion of the family.

The other related situation to this are owners that are frightened of dogs or even hate dogs and get a dog for protection purposes only. Never get a dog if you are afraid them or don't even like dogs. Fear must be overcome with gradual counseling and perhaps therapy overseen by a professional. These people have little or no concern for the dog's welfare and needs; he or she was purely for physical protection and not for love and companionship. When someone owns a dog, they might utilize them solely as a means of property protection; 99 percent of times, the dog is ignored, dissocialized, or abused, and trained to be vicious. Thus human's best friend will eventually become a danger to the individual, their family, and the public they were intended to scare off. If a person is afraid of a dog, why would they assume the dog will become an integral part of the family? If someone loves their companion animal, they many times will instinctively watch over and protect their family in the event they are faced with imminent danger.

You can be certain that the caring guardian is extra proud of them. However, folks in fear of a dog and see them as property security will never appropriately tend to the needs of an animal and the dog becomes an "it" and destined to live a short, horrible existence.

Humans are hugely responsible for our animal companion's demise. What type picture is the public painting for our children? What if there are several pit bulls chained to trees day after day in back of a wooded property, only minimally cared for by their apathetic owner(s) and a child daycare is right next door visible to it all? What are you teaching a child right off? You are automatically conditioning a child to fear dogs and to regard them as are mere property—an implied threat to humans. If you think this is proper mentoring, you are truly not improving their state and/or helping to change the public's opinion on animal rights. Our examples, positive or negative, of how we treat and care for animal companions will be a direct influence on our youth, which will imprint lasting values on a child into maturity. We must police ourselves and make conscious and sound decisions when considering placing a living, breathing being into our homes—a domestic companion for life.

These are only a few examples of the many dismal situations a dog ends up in—especially those misinterpreted breeds, such as Pit Bull Terriers or Rottweilers. The objective for a safe and secure home is completely destroyed by basic incompetence. Confined dogs don't protect a darn thing! The dog won't have any purpose except for future neglect, abuse, or property status. Know what you are getting into and educate yourself fully on all aspects of animal companionship. Dogs are not inanimate things. You should never *own* a dog. A dog is supposed to be an additional family member. Dogs have a sense of pain, feelings, and emotions just as humans do—and we all need to consider these if and when we decide on adding on to the household. If you consider dogs to be property, don't get one. Get a hobby. Easy fix.

Five: The parent or child is allergic to dogs.

You'd be surprised by how many people get a dog—even though they suspect they may be allergic to them however—because their child really wants a puppy. Worse, parents believe the myth that there are hypoallergenic dogs designed for allergic folks. This has been disproved for quite some time by many reputable veterinarians and researchers. In this instance, you could easily opt to bring your child once or twice a week to a shelter to allow him to learn responsibilities and proper care for dogs. It would also teach him valuable lessons on the importance of adoptions, veterinarian care, spaying and neutering importance, etc. If you can't, perhaps a trusted friend or neighbor could assist. Then you can rest assured that he or she will learn proper values and the child can adopt a dog later in his life. Of course, if the child is allergic, you can teach him other ways to respect animals—domestic, farm, or wild. You don't need to have a dog if your health keeps you from getting one. Consider another animal to adopt or donate to worthy causes and continue to educate him or her on humane treatment of all animals. Dogs are not the only animals abandoned and in need of our rescue. Consider routing his or her attention in understanding all animals that are abused and neglected and are in need of assistance. Check your local shelters to see what other animals need fostering or support and perhaps you will find another wonderful friend!

There are thousands of reasons or situations that may hinder you from adopting a dog, but remember that dogs are social creatures that need attention, love, and a committed family. Just because a child says they want a dog does not require a parent to act on it. Consider all options that will both suit yours and the child's enrichment needs. I encourage parents to get their kids actively involved and educated on all animals—domestic, farm, and wild. There a dozens of healthy approaches parents can take to accommodate all situations. I love horses, but I don't go out and adopt one because I know that I can't take care of them appropriately. Parents should consider the same in this huge undertaking.

Dogs are not some haphazard pursuit. Unless you are prepared to accommodate those basic lifelong needs, a dog is not your answer. In 2010, I personally observed a significant number of puppies adopted or purchased by employees (including their family members and/ or relatives) and have given them away by one means or another—to friends, shelters or the pound. It's tough to hear a colleague brag about their wonderful new companion one day and a few

Dog lovers don't care if you don't adopt a dog. The issue comes when you adopt a dog you don't love!
V. Nunley

months later come right back around and ask if I know anyone who wants a dog. Puppies in this particular region are almost becoming a shuffling statistic! Most puppies I've encountered with sudden change of hearts have been Labradors, Shepherds, and pit bulls, but it happens with many of our breeds. We encourage folks to learn and grow with dogs, but everyone is not suited for dogs.

CHAPTER 7

A Brighter Look at the Big Boys when Considering Adoptions

Large

versus

 Small

It's all about the "large and in charge" this go round! "Da Big Dogs" are finally getting big praises for those who are looking to adopt a wonderful, loyal animal companion!

Folks, let's not always rule out medium to larger dogs when considering a new four-legged companion. Though those cute designers and toy dogs are exceptional, there are advantages and disadvantages to whatever size dog you may choose for your family. In this chapter, we will touch on some of the positives of these larger dogs. Here are the top ten advantages I've found through a survey of guardians living with larger mixed and purebreds:

1. You never have to worry about accidentally sitting on them or pinning them in the couch cushions. Like to see you smoosh an Irish Setter in your recliner!
2. They are easier to housetrain than small breeds! And, you can find the poop pronto! Since little guys are one of the most challenging dogs to housetrain, you may miss that little dried up puddle from Princess the Pomeranian under the china cabinet for a week. On the other hand, you will definitely find Gracie the Great Dane's pile of poop faster! Easy to spot—a quicker picker-upper!
3. Larger dogs tend to be more durable and not as easily injured (minus a few breeds, of course) through handling; enabling them to withstand Junior or little Suzie's roughhousing. Fewer trips to vet for broken bones!
4. Larger dogs come in all shapes, talents, and characteristics—especially if they are a mixed breed. They can be used for a variety of sport and agility events! I'm sure there are a few talented Petit Basset Griffon Vendéens as well!
5. Larger dogs are usually more adaptable to weather changes. A handful—such as greyhounds and Dane—has thinner coats, but they are the exception to the rule. Every condition has its exceptions.
6. The big guys are easier to find when hunting for them throughout your household—they won't be hiding in an open drawer or under the kitchen cabinets! More often than not, Rodney the Rottweiler will alert you far stronger and louder than Max the Maltese when accidentally left behind a closed door!

7. Larger dogs aren't as finicky for the most part—ever met a Chihuahua that wasn't hard to please?

8. Larger dogs will never have a Napoleon Complex! Neighbors will take heed to your giant Schnauzer breed automatically! They prove their worth automatically through their size.

9. Small dogs are many times referred to as the "yappy and snappy" while the medium to large guys get the bad rap! In fact, most guardians actually allow little guys to get away with bad behavior—and seldom employ corrective training on unwarranted domination/disrespect issues. With the bigger guys, behaviors are modified more rapidly than for their tiny counterparts.

10. Large and medium breeds are sadly more often the last pooch to be picked at the pound. These guys may not even get a fair shake in potential adoption process and will many times be overshadowed by the smaller guys when they can be easily revered as the most loyal and smartest dogs around! Let's take a look at the Top Ten Favorite Dogs surveyed by most of the canine community and by the AKC website (five out of ten are medium to large dogs.):

*Based on AKC Rankings in 2009 (**American Kennel Club Announces Most Popular Dogs—January 27, 2010**):			
Rank	**Breed**	**Rank**	**Breed**
1	Labrador Retriever	6	Boxer
2	German Shepherd	7	Bulldog
3	Yorkshire Terrier	8	Dachshund
4	Golden Retriever	9	Poodle
5	Beagle	10	Shih-Tzu

Half of those favorite breeds were large or medium! In fact, finding a mixed breed of those dogs is quite easy in many shelters today, which gives them an added bonus on the "smarts" scale! All dogs are terrific, of course, but don't rule out the big fellahs and give them a second look before you make your final decision. In fact, why not compromise. Adopt one small and one larger breed (mixed or pure) from the shelter or rescue organization! Dogs love companions to play with while you are out and they will have some other playmate to keep them entertained on those long workdays!

A "pair" in this case can beat out an "ace in the hole!"

CHAPTER 8

Designer or Devotion—Don't Allow Dollars to Override Your Dedication

Many people decide on an animal companion only for the status, image, or some other reason besides devotion and love. You may opt for that designer pooch, but you should never forget to consider all the implied tasks that come along with that newfound spotlight. Are you still going to be just as loving to Pierre or Princess even if he or she don't make the cut or placing? Or, will they be put aside or neglected for the other promising sibling next to him that may finally get you that long awaited best in show. Devotion and commitment to your dog is life-long—no matter the winnings or lack of.

It's a fact that many guardians breed and show dogs for mere profit, becoming absorbed in their own agenda or vanity and not focusing on the one who's winning all the trophies and money! Be wary of obsessive scheduling, overtraining, or abusive handling and do not let your greed, status, and bank account overrun your primary objective. Remember your dog's welfare. Be a proud guardian and handler of a champion agility contest winner or even that best in show, but be as proud of that dog that may not make the grade but continues to unconditionally love you.

Your dog is not there for your egotism. Though your dog may qualify to enter specific events and showings, it does not however, give you the right to hog the spotlight and forget the needs of your best friend! It is your obligation to Rover that you know and adhere to their specific limitations and health needs—how long your four-legged companion stays in the race—ensuring they live a long and productive life.

"Grooming… $300

Training…$800

Best-in-Show… $50,000

Best Friend…
      Priceless!"

Never do any tasks to the extreme, whether its dog shows, agility competitions, or herding and retrieving. Your dog is your best friend and wants to please you more than the public. He or she is giving his all for your attention and love. Reward, praise, and give plenty of rest periods and some extra lengthy cuddling times. Never let them feel that he or she is not your priority. Dollars mean nothing to Damien the Dandie Dinmont! Always keep your dog physically and emotionally conditioned. They are neither property nor an investment. They are loving companions throughout their lives.

CHAPTER 9

Common Sense Tips on Donating to Animal Welfare Organizations

"Agoraphobia" defined in Doggy Terms!

It has been an ongoing struggle to choose what organization to donate to for the simple fact that we know we must do something but just don't know who, what, where, or how to give our time and/or money. Never are we going to have enough time, energy, or funds to help everyone or make everyone happy, but just know these important considerations: Everyone is different. With this in mind, we all have different likes and personalities. This is good so that our differences make our donations diverse and spread out! One individual may have been affected by seeing animals exploited by circuses or the entertainment business and it influenced them to donate and/or become an activist while others saw an abandoned pooch in need of a warm, cozy bed.

Just have enough faith that there are a lot of people concerned. However, don't fall into the idea that someone else is already involved so I don't have to be. Then no one would get involved! Yes, it is the fault of people being irresponsible toward our animal companions—and we need organizations to step in and eradicate animal abuse.

Additionally, spread the word through educating the public on the wrongs and needs of our animals and someone will hopefully feel moved enough to assist. For now, let's focus on choosing and channeling your passion to do something. So, who do you help? Just pick a couple or three. Start locally—see what the community needs—and then if you have some left over, spread out to other more specific agendas. If you have Dobermans, perhaps donate to a Doberman rescue or if you don't have a preference, your local humane society or the ASPCA is a great start!

Two, know your limitation and know how much to give. I use this rule of thumb. If it is common to pay yourself first, then take a percentage of that and give it to something you are passionate about. It is imperative that you are healthy and can sustain yourself before you overextend on outside causes. If you can't take care of yourself, you do more harm and will ultimately suffer—never effectively helping humans or animals. I try to look at it the way a lot of folks do with faith-based organizations. I subtract what is required to pay all my bills and then figure a percentage for investing in the future welfare of others. Churches may set a "10 percent rule" while you may see you have a bit more to donate. Just figure out what your future is comprised of! Mine is continuing the animal species and their coexistence alongside their human companions. When I put that into the equation, I must set aside each month to organizations I wish to donate money and contribute my time and energy into that agenda. Your intent may be an extension to some other human organizations you give to.

Three, get involved if you don't have the funds. There are groups that spend their free time in the community and volunteer to build fences for dogs that have no play areas. Some groups assist with building shelters, distributing donated supplies and food, etc. I have a wonderful friend that I met many years ago when I was in the military and his faith has taught him that if you cannot give in monetary form, you should donate your time and resources you have available to the unfortunate (i.e. food, clothing, extra furnishings, etc). This could be practiced with animals as well. I have lived with that principle.

Before I was able to make monetary donations, I would donate refurbished doghouses or extra cans of dog or cat food or whatever I had when I was really strapped and without money. You can become really creative and volunteer with local animal rescue events or community drives and donate your time by temporarily fostering a furry friend! When I incorporate a couple of options into my daily routine, I find myself more diverse in my outreach rituals. Every little bit helps! Offer your neighbor a bag of dog food or a ride to the vet if they recently lost their job or vehicle and can't get Rusty to the veterinarian for his routine shots. Help install a dog door for the neighbor's pooch that is stuck inside or outside all the time and just needed someone to help for the moment. No act of kindness or assistance is too small! Just remember to not stop. Your assistance should be ongoing. It should become part of your routine—and know it is well worth it in the long run. Think outside the box and outside yourself, as I like to put it.

Do your research! How many times have I seen my own family members give to some organization and it is a scam? Do your homework and find out through websites, media, friends and colleagues so you can make an informed decision. Word of mouth is always a way to find out about a good local organization's needs and reputation. I try to go with the known ones. Investigate the group to ensure that they are helping animals and the donations are being used for the missions outlined—and not going into someone's pocket.

What we have learned here is that every little bit counts! Go ahead, see what's going on in your neck of the woods and if there is nothing needed there, and extend it to those who need your help. Our animal companions are depending on you!

CHAPTER 10

Doggy Daycare and Boarding Kennels—Go by choice, not chance!

Though horror stories have been publicized about the care and safety of different boarding kennels and doggy day care centers across the nation, there are several that truly take the time and effort to ensure your animal companion has a healthy and safe environment to stay in.

When you absolutely, positively can't bring your animal companions with you, here are some things you may want to think about when boarding your best friends:

- Check out the center well in advance before boarding your precious loved ones.
- What is their particular emphasis? Dogs? Cats? Exotic or equines?
- Make sure you go to a center that is designed for your companion in mind!
- If at all possible, find out from others how their past experience was in the particular establishment. Again, word of mouth is worth a million bucks!
- Internet forums, veterinarians, and local welfare organizations may have great recommendations as well. Beware of those groups that get kickbacks because they recommend a certain place!
- Remember, you go cheap, you get cheap. This doesn't mean you have to spend and a leg and a paw, but sometimes you get what you pay for. On rare occasions, even the expensive boarding places have not-so-good reputations.
- Do your homework and research any place you're going to leave your babies with. Do they have scheduled daily activities? Do they have individual and unique programs in place for those not-so-gregarious pooches?
- Check the qualifications and previous handling experience of the on-site staff.
- Check for organization, cleanliness, and nutritional guidelines of the establishment. Bring any special dietary or prescription needs with you and give written instructions to the caretakers that will care for your companions.
- If more than a few days, find out if there are programs that will accommodate your particular breed(s) interests.
- Check the facility's ability to handle multiple-companion families.
- Ensure your companions are current with all vaccines and medications.

- Check the facility's containment and enclosures. Ensure the grounds are free of vermin, insects, dirt and other dangerous materials that your curious animal may get into. Can your companion get out?
- Check ratio of staff to number of animals on premises.
- Read up on all the guidelines and ensure they will keep your dogs together and free from harm or mating with other dogs.
- Check if the facility has up-to-date technological advances that will aide you in periodic monitoring of your furry friends. This is a wonderful new breakthrough that will help to ease your worries while missing your loved ones on those long business trips.

These tips are designed with your pooches in mind! Everyone hates to leave their loved ones in someone else's care, but we know it is sometimes a necessity. Consider your companions just as you would if you were leaving your two-legged loved ones in another's care. You want the best quality of care to minimize the stress on both you and your companion animals.

CHAPTER 11

"Project Groom-Way"—Choosing the Right Groomers

Some folks love to clean and care for their "youngins" themselves while there are those who decide to shell out the extra funds and give their pooches the spa treatment, so to speak. Groomers pop up out of nowhere and can be reputable or not. Follow a few simple tips to ensure that you pick the right outside facilities and groomers for taking care of your companion's grooming needs.

No one wants their pedigree pooches or diamonds in the rough to sport a dingy skin or coat. Have your companion looking spiffy enough to walk the runway—mixed or purebred, since they all are just as important. Remember that some breeds do not need over-grooming. You will be shelling out a lot of unnecessary funds if you are not careful. Dogs have natural oils that help protect their skin so over-bathing can cause skin irritations or hair loss. However, those brushes and combs are always great for massaging and eliminating excessive hair. Additionally, there are a lot of holistic oils and conditioners that are great for their skin and coat. Either way, consider a consult from your veterinarian before you go for extra grooming treatments. Professional groomers should know each breed's characteristics and specific needs. If they are reputable, you will have no problems. Here are some things I look for and you should as well:

(Note: Some of these considerations will look similar to choosing boarding facilities.)

- First, you need to ask around and get other guardians' suggestions. Most avid dog lovers will get the word out fast of the not-so-good groomers or let you know about the most reputable ones in town.
- If you're bringing your favorite canine to a facility, make a preliminary investigation of the facility and personnel before you drop off your companion. Check out all equipment that is used by private in-home groomers as well.
- Look for cleanliness, sturdiness, and safety of stations and equipment. Check for animal-safe and environmentally safe chemicals and products being used on your companion(s). Watch how equipment and/or items are cleaned, prepped, and stored for use on companion animals.
- Check for damaged, old, and outdated equipment and safety features to ensure your dog is safe from harm.

- Check tethering techniques and washbasins. Are dogs free from being accidentally strangled or unattended at any given time?
- Are heating and drying stations safe and timed, effective, warm, and free of debris? Check how close these machines are to your dog's level—too close could burn, too far could be nothing but cold air.
- Checks the length of time dogs are kept waiting in line and standing up on stations. Are there rest periods and pee breaks for more difficult grooms?
- Watch for unsafe cables and cords and check to ensure dogs are supervised and handled during the entire grooming process.
- Check out the groomer/handlers—both the in-home or outside facilities. Watch how they handle and control your companions that are being groomed.
- Check for the years of experience your groomer(s) have and type experience for different breed variations. Pay attention to handler/dog interactions.
- Check for certifications and requirements for companions to be up-to-date on shots and so forth. Do they require it and do they ask for documentation up front?
- Is the environment a friendly, inviting atmosphere? Do the owners and management handle conflicts and mistakes with genuine care and concern for you and your dog's welfare?
- Pay *very* close attention to nail-trimming equipment and procedures. This will usually make or break a particular establishment or groomer! If it is just an individual case due to whatever reason, notify management and see if there are other more experienced trimmers available.
- After you're comfortable with a place outside or a private in-home groomer, keep lines of communication open and inform groomers of any changes or updates in your companion's needs to maintain a healthy relationship between animals, their guardians, and groomers.

We want all our furry friends to have a positive experience that never risks physical or mental trauma to them. Guardians can find numerous resources by word of mouth, blogs, social networks, advice columns, TV, radio, community bulletin boards, and local shelters. Veterinarians have always been a great source of information. Guardians should take the time to explore all options for the safety and welfare of the fine companion friends.

CHAPTER 12

Summer and High Temperature Preventive Measures

I have highlighted some of the top concerns when it comes to dealing with the hot and humid season. My favorite vets around the county gave me some great tips and concerns when it came to companions dealing with the scorching temps we have in the South. High heat and summer festivities pose unique problems for our companion animals. We have to be on the lookout and take special precautions for these to ensure maximum health and safety while going through our typical routines this part of the year. Thanks and big shout-outs to the wonderful veterinarians that work hard to save and maintain our companion animals!

Here are some guidelines to live by while enduring sweltering weather conditions. Many are logical, but some may not be so common to novice guardians.

- Heat must be our first and foremost concern when it comes to domestic companions.

  o Specific breeds or those with special characteristics can be more susceptible to problems with exhaustion, strokes and worse, death during hot weather months.

  o Pooches with heavy muscling (pit bull terriers, boxers, bulldogs) and overweight dogs are predisposed to overheating. Large breeds also have a problem with quickly overheating due to their hearts pumping overtime to compensate for their larger stature.

  o Our furry companions who possess pushed-in faces, such as English and French Bulldogs, pugs, and many of the toy breeds have poor abilities in regard to dissipating heat. These dogs commonly have their snouts pushed in. We must take extra care since their breathing is somewhat labored due to their breed.

  o Be mindful of those dogs that are seen carrying their favorite tennis balls around all day. They too have a problem with overheating since their airway is partially blocked by the ball. They run back panting and huffing and can't get enough air for proper cooling. You need not overwork them on those activities. I know my Suzie is obsessed with her ball and doesn't want the other dogs to take it. So she holds it in her mouth all the time, waiting for me to throw it. I usually limit her playtime to early morning or sundown during the hot and humid times.

  o Cats and dogs left inside closed vehicles can be killed by excessive heat during the summer. Even if guardians crack their windows, the direct sun blasts through the windshield, turning the car into an oven, posing a huge threat to our loved ones. Think of it like a solarium. Dr. Brown, DVM, a local veterinarian says, "Even if the temperature drops as low as 75 degrees Fahrenheit, the inside of a vehicle can heat up to around 120 degrees Fahrenheit in less than twenty minutes. Your domestic companion can suffer heat stroke and die in less than one hour."

o Another killer to our animal companions is being chained up outside in the hot sun with no shade or water. Aside from chaining being cruel, folks will inadvertently place metal or flimsy plastic bowls that are easily tipped over near their animal that is chained, and ultimately the dog goes without any water for hours on end. Additionally, water will heat up in these shallow bowls to make the water almost unpalatable! Guardians must also be aware that water becomes stagnant after some period of time if bowls are not cleaned out regularly. Thus, you expose your companion animals to various bacterial infections and diseases—especially to weakened immune systems.

o Our thick furry animal companions are not the only ones at risk during hot weather conditions. Those with little to almost no hair will develop hotspots and skin conditions that can burn just as human skin will. These designer breeds tend to have systems that are delicate. Be considerate to all breeds during the hot and humid weather conditions and allow them inside to allow them an adequate shaded area with plenty of water. Don't forget to clean them regularly!

o Signs of heat stroke or exhaustion in our furry friends include excessive panting, collapse, slower gait or pace, dark red gums, very little urine production (many times dark yellow or brown and highly concentrated, just like in human heat stroke victims). Animals will frequently have a body temperature rise above 108 degrees Fahrenheit. This can lead to permanent organ damage, such as kidney and brain damage, clotting, and death! Some things guardians can do if they find any animal in such distress: immediately cool them in a pond or pool and call a veterinarian and transport the animal there as soon as possible. Cooling by water baths or fans, and towels immersed in cold water, can also help. A veterinarian should always be involved to ensure no permanent damage has set in or to prevent further complications. Heat stroke and injuries due to excessive heat are always avoidable. Keep fresh cool water on hand and give it to your companions freely. Keep companions wet and cool during your summer walks as well.

- Keep sunscreens, insect repellants, oils, and any oily skin products out of reach of animals.

  o As labels will indicate on these items, these products can cause various stomach irritations and central nervous system depression. Dogs by nature lick and sniff! Oils that are inhaled can cause aspiration within the lungs, resulting in pneumonia. DEET in many repellants is known to cause neurological problems in our animal friends. Some signs of toxic ingestion of these products are weakness, depression, coma, respiratory failure, and death. These items are labeled as harmful to animals, so avoid having them around. Consider natural repellants or make sure that your companions do not have access to unnatural ones. Check labels carefully.

- Alcoholic beverages should never be given to animal companions.

  o Many of the same symptoms that were outlined above include dehydration, lethargy, and severe depression. Dogs and cats are mammals so alcohol will act much as it does in humans, but it is more harmful to their smaller stature. Avoid alcohol at all costs!

- Lighters, matches, and other incendiary devices are another threat.

  o Matches contain chlorates that may damage circulation, breathing, skin, or the gastrointestinal system. This information can be found on the Material Safety Data Sheets (MSDS) of each of these compounds. You can find more information on them on the Internet through OSHA and the Centers for Disease Control. Also, your local veterinarian has plenty of factsheets on these topics. Read them thoroughly!

  o Inhalation and absorption of butane and lighter fluids could cause pneumonia from aspiration.

- Fireworks are not only dangerous and have dangerous properties—they can physically and mentally traumatize our companion animals.

  o Avoid taking them to large firework celebrations. Have areas that your companion can hide in from possible neighborhood fireworks if your animal has a propensity to be traumatized by them.

  o Pick up wasted fireworks in your yard. Debris from fireworks can also be harmful and the sticks can lodge in the esophagus.

  o Fireworks contain high concentrates of minerals, metals, nitrate, and arsenic—all toxic to our companions.

  o If ingested, vomiting, diarrhea, jaundice, tremors, or seizure could occur. Contact your veterinarian immediately should any of these conditions appear. Also contact them for further guide in fireworks dangers.

- Don't overfeed or continuously change your companion's diets.

o   Changing food can result in bouts of diarrhea and indigestion. This is true any season. If you don't believe this, spend some time around your loved ones and change their diets even once. I promise you will know it as soon as you lay next to them that evening! All dog guardians are remotely aware of this and will warn new care providers of this simple fact.

o   Veterinarians can further brief you on dangerous foods, such as chocolate, grapes, yeast dough, and onions. These are some examples of additional foods your animal should avoid.

o   Some of our people food should be avoided when the proper nutrients are not provided in them. Some advocates support homemade raw diets that provide for the nutritional health of our canines. There are particular recipes designed with your pooch in mind! Venture out and explore some of the holistic preparations and medications that are equally great for our pooch pals.

o   Greasy foods should be avoided. These cause digestive issues as well. Too much grease is unhealthy for any mammals!

o   Reputable veterinarians may advise against bones due to them breaking and lodging into an animal's digestive tract. You will notice animals getting a delayed reaction should a blockage occur. Obstructions will lead to your companion being unable to eat or severe abdominal pains. Plus they can inadvertently rupture the stomach linings. Many surgeries are a result of this one simple situation that could have been avoided. You don't eat bones so neither should your companions. They are not wild animals. Your hounds are not wolves; they are domesticated and have different dietary needs. Additionally, summer weather will cause bacterial growth to accumulate faster on those greasy, meaty bones they carry around for hours on end.

- Pig ears and rawhides are not always a good treat.

  o These items could easily become a breeding ground for bacteria and insects. Summer months can accelerate these issues and cause problems later. Though some veterinarians find them safe, many of my animal rights advocates avoid them. It's basically a split opinion as to the safety and health of these items—you may opt to seek your veterinarian on this subject matter. Pick up one of those grungy leftover rawhides form the floor and decide whether you would put it in your mouth. Rawhide and pig ears can lead to gum disease as well. They're not easily digestible. There are several chew toys on the market that are safe, washable, and allow hours of fun.

- Perform frequent "landmine" patrols of your areas!

  o Feces harbor several bacterial and insect accumulations and is further exacerbated by the hot and humid temperatures.
  o Consider doing more clean-up during these hot months. Insects and larvae can find refuge in waste and come into contact through dog and cat paws.
  o Cut your grass! You can't see accumulations of waste if your grass is knee high. This is another breeding ground for insects to fester and make a home. It is easier to catch the old feces you may have missed if it's more visible—thus preventing waste from coming into your house unintentionally. Dogs love to roll around in lush lawns, but when it gets too tall, you now have Binky rolling in piles of waste infested with all types of unwanted contaminants.
  o Additionally, those dogs that have problems with eating their feces will have more health problems. Talk to your veterinarian on this particular problem so they can recommend some ways to avoid these complications.

Guardians should always police their yards and play areas for waste—regardless of weather conditions. Try to be more diligent during these hot and humid times.
o   Rainy seasons will also become problematic with excess waste in yards, so pick up and discard of waste as soon and as frequently as possible. Wet waste will become moldy and bring additional problems into your dog's life and environment.

- Chem-lights and glow in the dark jewelry can be harmful.

    o   Please get a copy of the MSDS on these items and read the labels carefully! Cats primarily will see these items as a novelty to play with since they are colorful, shiny, and glow. They all have a propensity to cause skin irritations upon contact.
    o   Though many are not considered toxic, stomach and digestive problem could still occur.
    o   Rinse your companion's mouth and offer plenty of liquid and safe treats to allow bad tastes or foul liquids to pass quicker.
    o   Plastic pieces broken or chewed off can result in blockages as well.

All these summer and hot temperature situations are almost all avoidable by responsible guardians. Take extra precautions with your companions during these risky seasons. Your best friends will be thankful for it and will have fewer complications.

CHAPTER 13

Cold Weather Safety Tips

Although many of our domestic friends have fur, dogs and other animals can still suffer from frostbite, hypothermia, and dehydration—and ultimately die in the below freezing temperatures. We seem to forget that some animals may not be prepared for unusual cold spells. This includes neighboring wildlife when water sources freeze and they have no way to hydrate properly. Cold temperatures are an extreme hardship for domesticated dogs left outside by uncaring owners. They often go without adequate food, water, shelter, or medical care. This winter, be a guardian to your animal companions and do not forget that they are out in the harsh elements.

When the temperatures drop, it's important to remember your companion's welfare as you do your own. Consider these safety measures when protecting animal companions during the cold winter months.

Bring them inside!

Think of those children (puppies and kittens) stuck out there. Our elderly animals, small animals, and dogs with short hair (i.e. some hound breeds, pit bulls, Rottweilers, Dobermans, Greyhounds, and Great Danes) are particularly susceptible to the elements. Short-haired little guys will also benefit from warm sweaters or coats when taking them on those extended walks. I personally recommend all dogs have access to the indoors—regardless of breed. Give them a dog door, you give them an option!

A slight increase in food portions in cold weather is helpful.

In cold weather, animals burn more calories to maintain warmth. Don't get carried away, but allow a bit of extra portion to provide for warmer conditions. Ensure that all shots and preventive medications are current. Check regularly if your companion animals are free of internal parasites that can rob them of vital nutrients. If the immune system goes down, the threat goes up exponentially!

Consider all animals during the cold weather season.

Wild animals and strays will be forever grateful from your hospitality. Many areas have become overpopulated with manmade structures and buildings that aren't animal-friendly. Gathering food becomes harder for the wildlife and strays. This is definitely true for feral cats. Even deer or other wild animals get caught up between the city limits with no place to find shelter. Take stray animals inside until you can find their guardians—or take them to an animal shelter. If strays are wild or unapproachable, provide food, water, and a simply constructed shelter as a minimum.

Some country dwellers may consider constructing some man-made squirrel shelters or small wooden coves for animals that may be stranded along their wood line, looking for a safe place out of the harsh elements. Provide a small doghouse or cat shelter filled with warm bedding for those you may find around abandoned lots and/or call your local humane society for assistance in trapping them and getting them indoors. We always want to take into account our companions, but try to remember the strays and wildlife!

Additionally, slow down and be mindful of deer and other wildlife that come out winter seasons! Some animals roam more frequently in the cooler season. Consider your speed this winter to avoid animal casualties as much as possible.

Don't allow your domesticated companions to roam about unattended outdoors.

In cold weather, cats frequently climb under hoods of cars to be near warm engines. Inattentive motorists can accidentally injure or kill an animal attempting to escape the cold when they start their vehicles. A simple preventive measure is banging on your vehicle hood before starting the engine to ward off any living creature that may have found a temporary safe haven there. It's common for animals—especially cats—though other small wild creatures may do this as well. Take care and use extra precautions to avoid injuries or death to all living animals.

If you live in areas that use salt on the ground, thoroughly clean off your companion's underbody, feet, and legs after they come in from the sleet or snow.

Salt may not be a concern here in the South, but folks that live in chilly towns may want to consider the tons of salt public workers put out during the snowy months. Salt and other chemicals can make animals sick if too much is ingested. Cats are especially susceptible to this because they are prone to constant licking and cleaning themselves.

Antifreeze is our companion's enemy—and highly toxic to our animal friends!

Consider purchasing the less toxic antifreeze made with propylene glycol instead of ethylene glycol, which can kill animals even in small doses. Check the labels and find the brands safe for animals. There are some marketed now so be a diligent guardian and look out for your companion's safety when choosing antifreeze brands. Animals are attracted to antifreeze for its sweetness, so clean up spills quickly, and buy brands with a bitter agent "Denatonium Benzoate" property found on the MSDS labeling.

If you have an outside breed that enjoys the colder temperatures (i.e. Chows, Malamutes, etc.), ensure they have adequate shelter.

Always know your specific breed tolerances and take care in the length of time you leave them out. Do your homework. Most domesticated dogs need to come inside below a certain temperature. All your doghouses should be made of wood and preferably insulated and positioned in a sunny location during cold weather. The plastic ones do nothing for insulation or heat retention. Raise the house several inches off the ground, and put a flap over the door to keep out cold drafts and melting snow or ice. Make sure the openings are leaned slightly down so they don't fill with water. This is a very common mistake for guardians. Use straw (not pine straw) or cedar shavings for bedding. Never use rugs and blankets as bedding because they will get wet and freeze. Don't have the doghouses for cold weather protection too large. Consult one of the reputable welfare organizations as to the proper size. You can have large doghouses, but for getting cozy and warm, they need a house that can hold in heat—not too small, but large enough to stand up and turn around. Then they can curl up and utilize some of their body heat within an enclosed area.

Consider providing water to wildlife in your neighborhoods and back yards.

Provide a source of water for the area wildlife for those who may have a difficult time finding drinking water during winter months. On those below freezing days, remember to break the top layer of ice so they can have access to the water beneath. Do this at a minimum of two times a day—preferably more. It won't do any good if they can't access the water!

Many humans enjoy feeding the ducks and geese, depending on their location. Avoid the typical bread or corn you usually opt to feed them. These foods provide very little in nutritional value for wintertime eating. The best thing to feed two-legged, feathery friends during the winter is dry cat food or dog food. The birds love it—and the percentage of fat in kibble will certainly help them stay warm as well as replenishing the water-repellent oil in their feathers.

CHAPTER 14

Fencing and Containment Safety Issues at Home—Do's and Don'ts to Live By

Consider a few quick tips when constructing or designing proper containment for your animal companions. Safety is always number one. You should also keep in mind the overall welfare and quality of life can be greatly improved when considering your pooch's protection and security around your establishments. Through numerous rescues and conversing with fellow activists, I have found some common issues.

When thinking of containment, consider the breed type. Some animals have a tendency to climb or jump while others are diggers.

- Always consider the thickness—not just the height of your dog. This will play an important factor in what type of fencing you go with.
- Seek advice from those who have adopted your particular breed or ask a friendly animal rights advocate or vet for special requirements if needed.
- Allow space for your dog to exercise and play with plenty of shade and shelter to provide security from the elements. Clear out any debris or dangerous items that may be in your yard and avoid any electric cables or fuel lines.
- Consider doghouses mounted to your house with dog door access into the dog-friendly section of your house. I do this and it works great! This also helps to hide the dog door entrance into your house to avoid intruders using it as an easy way to get in your house if you have any large dogs. I constructed a doggie breezeway by extending the doghouse and have two flaps to create minimize heating bills and reduce some of the bugs coming into the house. Make it at least as long as your longest dog. I have a Great Dane in my crew so mine sticks out about four feet.
- Spay or neuter your companions! You'll be amazed how well this helps with some of the escape artists who are looking for a new mate! This will tone down some of those urges to get out as well. Some will still want to go out and explore so don't think this is a 100 percent solution. Regardless, spaying and neutering is encouraged for several other reasons.
- Use vertical fencing slats that are butted right up to each other to help to reduce risk of injury to your companions.

  o Privacy fencing on at least three sides of your dog's play area will also help to minimize some of the overactive barkers. Have one side visible to an area that is predominately doggie-free. This will give your pooches a whole area to look at the scenery. This reduces some of the boredom, giving him or her some new things to peer at on the outside.

- Avoid short, wide-spaced picket fences.

    o If you use something similar to this type of fence, ensure they have no sharp tips or slats are no wider than an inch or two apart (less if a smaller dog) and make them very tall. Dogs also tend to get pinned between picket fence slats so avoid spaces between the slats so it cannot allow any part of your dog to become trapped.
    o With these types of fences, it is imperative to have them larger than what a dog can stand, leap, or jump across. Dogs have been impaled with this type of fencing. I do not recommend this type!

- Some opt to go the electric route. Many are divided on the safety concerns. If you use electric fencing, have an expert install it or be well-versed on installation and electricity safety. Some advocates shun this altogether. Some find these helpful for more difficult behaviors. Usually the bad habits will subside after a few times of coming into contact with the wire, but only use it as a last resort.
- I don't recommend underground fencing, but it may be suitable for certain breeds and should be used early in a dog's life. If they pass through the boundary, they may not be able to get back in! How long will you be gone that day?
- Properly install chain link fencing. Use chain link that is properly mounted and staked well under the ground to keep diggers from getting under.

o Use cement inlays or wire mesh a few feet linked at the base of the fence and going in about a foot or two. Then cover the area with soil or grass. This will help to avoid digging in those areas as well. Give them an alternate digging play area to deflect their attention away from the fence border.

o Check your fence perimeter regularly and repair any weakened areas.

• Never leave collars or harnesses on dogs that look over or can reach across your fence.

o Dogs will get hung by collars. If you insist on having a collar for their tags, etc. try using "break-away" style collars for dogs that are left inside fencing when you are away. Well trained dogs don't require this extra precaution, but those with little or no training may opt to do this.

o Use regular collars when you are walking or taking your dog somewhere.

o Have your dog micro-chipped and ensure they have up-to-date records—on the premises and easily accessible.

• Never leash or tether a dog inside a fenced area.

o If you are doing this, it means you don't have proper fencing in the first place! Fix the fence and avoid long-term costs and dangers in the future.

o It is highly recommended that dogs should not be tethered for any extended period. This is discussed more in the chapter "Chains Always Lead to Pain."

CHAPTER 15

Introducing Collars and Leads to Your Companions

Depending on the type, breed, and training level of the dog, you may opt to use specific types of collars and leads to accommodate your particular needs. Let us centralize our discussion on garden-variety dog-guardians and give some common-sense approaches to choosing collars and leads. Experts may have other options available, but I will give the public a few simple suggestions.

It is always a good idea to consult your veterinarian on the proper fit and type that may be recommended for your specific breed if you are unsure of any situation that may come up. Maybe Junior was put into your household at eight weeks old. Perhaps the little puppy is Boxer, Labrador, or a mixed little fellah rescued from the humane society. Either way, many guardians will wait and not place collars on the little tyke until they actually take the little one out for his first walk. This may be a bit late and put a strain on your pleasant walking experience. Let's look at a few suggestions:

1. Place a collar on your puppy or dog as soon as possible and under visual supervision only! Initially, dogs need to get used to the feel of a collar and leashes so that they don't feel intimidated by them. Let it be a positive tool and make him feel it is a rewarding opportunity as well. Use lightweight leashes at first. Use the collars with the plastic snaps and never a buckle-type collar during training. Buckles have a tendency to inadvertently readjust and tighten—and may cause your dog to choke to death! Leashes initially should be short leads so they may let them follow the pup around with not too much interference and in your presence only. Never leave a new pup unattended in the house or yard with a collar and/or leash. You must first train your companions and dog-proof your house and yard before leaving collars on them if they are temporarily out of your site. I prefer to never leave them on unsupervised. I implore you to microchip your new companions and have proper fences constructed.

2. Never use choke chains or spiked correction collars on any dogs—and never use them on new puppies! Activists recommend more positive training techniques and these usually fall under negative reinforcement. You will find trainers for specific purposes—law enforcement and protection services—use these on dogs that have better muscling and for short training sessions. Commonly, those who opt for the humane way of training will not consider these. However, if they are used, we prefer that they are used properly. This can become a danger if this is a practice.

Puppies always need to be started out with a more positive approach—and never choke chains.

3. Harnesses are great if fitted and used properly for the particular breed and level of training. Again, this is dependent upon the owner's tastes. Many will only recommend harnesses, but some opt to stick with traditional collars. The better trained your dog is, the easier it is to use conventional collars. As for the obedient ones, a typical wide leather or nylon collar is fine. Again, buckle collars are never recommended. Harnesses may be the best approach for some hyperactive dogs, such as terriers and working dogs. Houses with multiple dogs that are very active and possess destructive behaviors may not be suitable for harnesses. These guardians may opt for traditional collars during supervised sessions only. Unless your dogs are well trained, harnesses should never be left on if you are not present. Active or curious dogs can get tangled or choked by those types. Also many guardians find the rambunctious ones in their family pack may assist in chewing them off for them. Consult your veterinarian, a reputable organization, or an activist for proper fit and comfort for the dog. Always check the fit regularly since young dogs grow out of them rather quickly.

4. Most activists (including me) encourage guardians to take all collars off of all unsupervised dogs inside or out—regardless of type. This includes puppies and extremely mischievous dogs until you or the trainer is back within eyesight. Dogs can easily get into things and choke themselves on unusual things, such as tree branches, fences and containments, timbers sticking out of sheds, chair railings, ironwork, pipes, etc. There are all types of dangers that can occur. If you have a very docile and content dog that lounges around on the front porch all day, then it may not be a problem. Additionally, those who have a family member at home all the time will probably not have a problem with collars on their dogs all the time either. Those who live alone or families where everyone works long hours may decide it is too much a risk for their curious hounds. Have your proper documentation available

should anyone ask if your certifications and shot records are up to date. Have them easily accessible and available to sitters should you not be there for their presentation to officials. It should go without saying, if collars are not on your dog inside your yard, you should have a durable fenced in area and up-to-date records easily accessible for local authorities.

5. Self-adjusting or slip collars (choke chains) are never to be used in combination with temporary tethering to a fixed object. This could ultimately choke a dog and lead to death. Never use these types—even on unsupervised dogs—tethered or not!

Always use a positive, humane approach in equipment and training for your four-legged companions.

CHAPTER 16

Chains Always Lead To Pain!

Many activists and animal welfare groups have repeatedly made clear the cruelties of chaining/tethering dogs. As a fellow activist, I side with those groups. Countless documents show the extreme dangers of tethering our companion animals.

In this segment, I outline the negative impacts tethering has on our canine companions. The first thing we need to recognize is how organizations define chaining or tethering. According to animal advocates and national organizations (HSUS), this term refers to "the practice of fastening a dog to a fixed/stationary object, such as a stake, tree, fence, etc. as a means to control the animal. These terms (tethering) have been separated and not ever referred to dogs that are being walked on a leash."

Continuous tethering poses a threat to a dog's physical and mental livelihood. Every reputable organization has stated that the practice is inhumane and a threat to not only the dog's safety but to humans that may come into contact with them. Although many areas are now banning tethering, chaining dogs is still legal and prevalent in many counties across the nation. We must look at encouraging our representatives to ban these cruelties for the sake of our companions.

Why is tethering so inhumane? Dogs have a need to be social with humans and other animals. A dog kept chained in one spot for days or even hours on end can be compromised mentally and physically. Continuous chaining can cause an otherwise playful, docile, or friendly dog to become neurotic, unpredictable, anxious, aggressive, and depressed—much like if a human was confined in such a manner for a long period of time. Many experts compare long-term tethering to inmates being confined in isolation for extended periods. Though many cannot agree to the exact time it takes, I would conclude that if one wanted to know how long it would take a dog to become completely unbalanced, we could see how long one of us would break in such conditions. Dogs are mammals. Though they are configured and wired differently with limited cognitive abilities, one could just watch his or her social interaction and know they have a brain and can feel pain and experience other emotions similar to us humans. If this were not true, we wouldn't be seeing all these research groups testing them! It is a well-known fact that researchers whose physiological makeup is as close as possible to that of humans to test new medicines and behavioral theories. Dogs are mammals therefore have similar makeup of humans just as apes, chimps and many other mammal species. With this assumption in mind, the dog is one of many animals subjected to this inhumanity. Logically one can conclude that if a dog has some remote similarities to humans, they will have an adverse reaction as would humans subjected to long-term chaining/tethering. Though this argument has been recognized by reputable organizations, many will discount the fact that dogs possess any feelings and tethering is of no threat to their behavior. Folks that believe such an abomination must have never interacted with man's best friend or are apathetic to the notion altogether.

Let me give you a mental picture in regard to the physical effects on our animal companions tethered for long periods of time. Without being scientific, one can see the physical harm it does to dogs. Just walk through a neighborhood and observe one dog that has been chained for days, months, or even years (though it would be unimaginable). Dogs that are chained for an indefinite time will show visible signs of trauma. They may have sores from collars or chains wrapped around their necks, rubbing their skin raw. As they continuously try to escape from the unwarranted confinement, they struggle and their skin will become irritated and infections can set in. They will also show visible sores, skin trauma, and abrasions. Dogs can be attacked by insects and other airborne elements from which they have no escape. Many dogs that are chained up for long periods are also neglected by their "owners." We see these types of guardians represented by this terminology since they would never be labeled as guardians if they allowed such treatments to their best friends. Outside, alone, and defenseless, they can be subject to attacks by other animals with no way to escape. Their inability to protect themselves will allow other predators—even humans—to harm them. Those afraid of dogs may taunt, throw rocks, hurl sticks, or commit other abusive acts toward defenseless dogs. Dogs are easy targets for other animals, insensitive humans, and insects.

Additionally, owners who use choke chains or collars that are not periodically adjusted can find their loving companion choked with the collars embedded deep into their necks after long periods of time, causing extensive damage—some severe enough to never recover. Dogs can end up dying or being euthanized due to the neglectful acts of the owner. Injuries are more likely to occur with tethered dogs. Many believe owners who tether animals are predominately neglectful humans who spend less time checking and caring for the dog than those guardians who actually care for their welfare. The longer a dog is tethered, the more likely the dog is to be ignored and forgotten. I have watched neighbors having picnics and playing on their front lawns with their entire human family (including the children) while their faithful animal companion is chained up without a hope of participating in the festivities. These same neighbors boast how they love them and claim that the dog is part of their family.

Other physical issues come about when a dog is unable to reach food, fresh water, or shelter if those chains prevent them from reaching them. Many do not realize that dogs can get tangled from moving around as would come naturally. Suddenly, they cannot drink from a bowl or get to shade or shelter. Simple things, such as an unreachable, tipped over bowl or a tangled chain, go unnoticed by owners for hours upon hours as they are stranded from either the harsh elements, or left to die in the elements. The US Department of Agriculture (USDA) issued a statement in 1996, but people remain apathetic to the dangers.

On July 2, 1996, the Federal Register said, "Our experience in enforcing Animal Welfare Act has led us to conclude that continuous confinement of dogs by a tether is inhumane. A tether significantly restricts a dog's movement. A tether can also become tangled around or hooked on the dog's shelter structure or other objects, further restricting the dog's movement and potentially causing injury."

Dogs trapped on chains for ridiculous amounts of time can be easily linked to owners that become less and less involved. This has been a long-standing fact and proved time and again by the most reputable organizations—if people would only notice what is going on even in their own communities. The ASPCA and PETA have expressed to the public the dangers of long-term tethering for decades.

What about the mental and emotional trauma caused by long-term chaining? According to an excerpt by the Humane Society of the United States (HSUS), dogs are naturally territorial and are protecting a very limited area while tethered. If they are confronted with any perceived threat, they instinctively respond just as humans respond when backed into a corner—fight or flight. Since those who tether dogs have inadvertently taken away the flight option, they are forced to fight out of fear. The longer they are a chained, the more the dog will begin to perceive. A study published by the Journal of the American Veterinary Medical Association in September 15, 2000, reported that "17 percent of dogs involved in fatal human attacks were restrained on their owner's property." These numbers grow every year. Even if released from a chain after so long, a dog will be more prone to remain aggressive. Wouldn't you be a bit pissed off? Countless studies show that dogs are not much different from humans as far as being confined for excessive amounts of time; they become unpredictable and may become psychotic.

Dogs are also forced to urinate, defecate, eat, and sleep in the same area day after day. Many owners will clean these areas sporadically—or even completely ignore them—and a dog is forced to live around insects, bacteria, diseases that may cause worms, or infections resulting in a slow death since does these neglectful owners rarely seek veterinary care for them. Does one have to even bring up the discomfort this living, breathing creature feels day after day?

Dogs on pulleys find themselves in the same predicament. The owners slowly forget they are there and become are eventually forgotten. Tethers on pulleys may become rusted and inoperable—leaving a dog stranded in the middle of the yard. And I can almost guarantee that those pulleys will get stuck in the middle of the blazing heat where your poor companion is stuck unable to reach food, water, or shelter. Thus the cruel cycle begins again.

Many groups and activists teach individuals on the proper care of their companions and a few simple guidelines to prevent this cruel practice. HSUS, ASPCA, and PETA agree that dogs should at least be kept

"He is your friend, your partner, your defender, your dog.
You are his life, his love, and his leader.
He will be yours, faithful and true to the last beat of his heart.
You owe it to him to be worthy of such devotion."
—Author unknown

indoors at night, brought on frequent walks for exercise, and be provided with adequate attention, food, fresh water, and regular veterinary care. A dog needs social interaction to help maintain his or her overall mental health and well-being. If housed outside for even a temporary time, look into constructing suitable pens with adequate square footage to roam and play in. Consider the elements and provide protective shelter within the enclosures. Though some may or may not agree, my thoughts are to allow dogs inside at their leisure—even if it's in a limited area of your home—to give them a life of happiness and security. No one requires that you go to the extent that I do (i.e. dog doors attached to house, clean and roomy areas, sleeping in the room), but put yourself into your dog's place. Would you want to be stranded, tied to a tree or stake for hours on end without proper care or even a small glimmer of attention every day of your life? I have stressed time and time again—first the fence, then the dog!

Consider realistically if you have the time and proper environment for a newfound friend. I urge anyone considering adopting a dog (or any animal companion) to read and seek professional advice and training before you take in a new companion.

CHAPTER 17

Traveling with Your Companions in Vehicles

People will discover that their domestic companions either completely love or hate traveling in vehicles with you. For them, there is no "sometimes" or "I'm just not in the mood today" kind of thinking. Two of my dogs despise traveling, but the other three see it as an adventure. I have to tackle both situations. Either way, here are some helpful tips in vehicle transportation.

First, try to start when they are puppies. If you didn't have this luxury—or you still have to get them over their fears and anxiety—try taking short trips to get them used to traveling. Reward and praise them excessively each step of the way. Gradually let them get used to longer trips before you head into cross-country trips. Sometimes you may have to enlist the help of your vet for meds to calm them down. There are also some holistic alternatives if you read up on the subject more extensively. Some have too much anxiety and might need additional support. I also try to travel with someone they like so they can be consoled throughout the trip. This helps to minimize some of the stress.

Multiple companion parents may opt for their dogs to travel together unless they are going on short visit to the vet or pet store. This way, they have each other to feel safe and secure. ASPCA-approved (or other major organizations) carriers keep them safe from being knocked around in the vehicle when turning corners or in sudden stops. Covering crates also helps for some guardians although one side should be a little open to allow your dogs to look outside or at you, depending on the position. They are naturally curious, but they need to feel safe and secure. Make the crates tall enough for them to stand up and turn around, but not too big to defeat the purpose of them being secure in the vehicle. Carriers must be properly secured. A simple fix could be securing the carrier with tie-down straps. You may be a terrific driver, but others on the road may not be.

For cats, a carrier is a must. There is no way around it. Most cats travel pretty well in carriers. Never travel with a cat outside a carrier! Take cats in carriers to and from vet offices, short trips, long trips, and all trips!

Make plenty of rest stops. Carry dry food and water that will sustain your companions for longer durations. Avoid feeding your animals while moving. If you are traveling for more than a day, make the feeding stops longer. Stop at a safe rest stop, feed your dogs, exercise them, and allow them to go before loading back up. Never allow a dog off of a leash in an unknown area since unknown dangers may lurk nearby. Rest stops tend to be near highways and your dog may run into speeding vehicles that are unaware of your pooch. Multiple dogs may need to be exercised separately, depending on levels of training.

Never haul dogs in the back of an open-bed pickup. Though laws in some counties do not prohibit such a mode of transportation, it is highly recommended for the safety of your companion that this alternative should never be used. Counties that allow open-bed transport have specific guidelines for proper tethering. Beds can be slippery or hot, which can cause trauma to your dog—never allow your dogs to ride in this fashion. To avoid any risk of injury, purchase a secure carrier approved by a national organization and use tie downs to anchor it to the bed. Consider the weather conditions and take short trips. Small carriers could be like an oven on particularly hot days. I recommend a partially wired cage in which airflow is maximized. All trips should be short-term in an open bed. Any vehicles used to transport dogs on longer trip need to be covered from the elements and have properly sized crates for each dog. For sedans and so forth, seatbelt restraints are great for single-dog families. For trips with multiple domestic companions, crates and carriers are the only way to go safely unless you have absolutely perfect trained pairs that will stay seated that long. We all have allowed our pooches to sit with us on the passenger seat. Experts will tell you that dogs should always be restrained or crated. An approved crate is the only way to go.

Watch for slamming car doors! I can't tell you how many injuries occur—and sometimes even death—with our companions and car doors. Guardians get out their vehicles and forget that Buster is right behind them, trying to see what's going on since you're going out there! Getting in or out of a vehicle, you need to be very cautious if your dog or any animal is riding unsecured. Even the best pooches get curious and want to run out unexpectedly. Newer vans can pose problems with the slow automatic closings. These are potentially very dangerous to pooches moving around inside your vehicle. Sometimes dogs don't realize doors are still closing and can get pinned in the mechanisms. Small dogs are especially at risk. Some folks never look to see if little Buffy, the Bichon Frise, is safely away from automatic doors. Please be especially careful in these situations. Automatic lift gates are also a huge danger. Be wary of any automatic devices when it comes to your companion's safety!

Ensure that all your companions are up-to-date on their shots. Carry copies of your companion's records and keep all tags and collars on pets when traveling long distances. Guardians and vets recommend micro-chipping your dogs for extra security. Have visible collars on your pooches for long trips. Check all equipment, leashes, crates, and packed items prior to leaving. A checklist is always helpful since they have unique needs.

CHAPTER 18

Hound-Proofing Your Haciendas!

I've been approached by many of my animal-fanatic friends on the subject of hound-proofing their premises. These tips are for the owners who cannot watch over their "rambunctious Rovers" twenty-four-seven. They look at your household as full of designer chew toys. Perhaps this isn't for the perfectly trained darlings that never make a mess of things in "Martha Stewart" homes. Canines and felines can pose particular risks to themselves and/or your household.

Let us delve into a few suggestions that will ease some of headaches up the road. Nothing is foolproof! Since many groups have unique behaviors, we cannot predict every situation. Cats have unique particulars as well. I represent a household with extremely spoiled terrors that look upon life and my house as their environment to rule. First and foremost, animals usually have short attention spans and bore easily. They have physical and social needs just as you do. Second, depending on their background, health, pedigree (or lack of), or home life, your animal companion may need specific adaptations. You may want to seek a specialist or vet for these unique problems. The less time you have to spend with your four-legged friends, the more you may want to adapt their living space. The tips are things I've done to help to live harmoniously with my five four-legged companions. Some may seem extreme, but you can modify as you see fit.

Financially prepare yourself to maintain a healthy, happy environment. This may seem trivial but if something is ruined because of your companion, are you going to go off the chain? Will you adapt and overcome? Replacing items may be costly if you don't prepare for puppyhood and untrained dogs. The more you consider your companions in your household purchases, the better you may be down the road.

Flooring should be non-porous, stain resistant, preferably non-slip, and have very little carpeting. This has saved me a bunch of heartache. I recommend wood flooring and tile wherever your dogs travel within the house. Other durable flooring is perfectly fine. I have a few strategically placed, heavy-grade, non-slip area rugs and washable floor mats on my tile and wood flooring. Hard surface floors help with shedders as well. Shedding hair can be easily picked up afterward and your cleaning is cut in half with less hairy buildup that rugs commonly encounter. Carpets are hair magnets! If you choose carpeting and can't live without them, consider them in rooms less traveled in. The materials, pile, grade, and the stain resistance of the carpet should be factor as well. This makes for easier cleaning and less strain on your body and wallet!

Furnishings should be durable, stain-resistant, and adaptable to the dogs. If your dogs are living side-by-side with you, spend wisely and with a long-term durability in mind. Leather, microfiber, satins, or easily stained and porous materials should be avoided. Think of iron, metal or strong wooden legs on tables and furnishings instead of fabric-covered or delicate ones that may be tipped over or chewed up. Consider purchasing durable non-toxic, pre-treated sofas and futons—and definitely utilize coverings that compliment, not destroy the aesthetics of your household. I always place simple printed sheets or furniture spreads over my futon mattresses and couches. Even though I have pretty durable materials, I can easily take them off and clean them regularly. If and when those finicky relatives come over to visit, they can be taken off to impress them with your non-holey and non-hairy cushions! Cover, wash, and deodorize frequently with animal safe products and give them plenty of other chew toys to keep them occupied till you come home to clean up their mess. Consider low-to-the ground furnishing if you desire the company of your cozy cuddly canines and felines (I've gone so far as to modify some myself). It will be advantageous for you and Bowzer in the long run! This can ease some of the hip, leg, and joint problems that some dogs encounter in later years. I use a very low box spring set on my bed along with steps in certain areas so that my loved ones have easier times to get up and down from their favorite lounges. This avoids a lot of broken legs and scratched up cushions in the future. Trust me!

Never leave untrained companion animals around rockers or collapsible furnishings—especially if they are small. Many animals have died as a result of getting caught between collapsible furnishings or inadvertently being crushed by rockers. Little paws or legs or even midsections can be pinned and crushed by unsuspecting rockers. Folding legs that don't lock in place are especially a hazard to our loved ones. They are accidents waiting to happen—avoid them in areas where your animal companions wander! If you have recliners and small pooches, check your seating and watch out for Trixie burrowing in the folds or in bulky cushions!

Knickknacks and decorative ornaments should be up on unreachable shelving or showcased in guarded cabinetry. Consider curios or tempered glass-encased cabinets. Ensure they are secured somehow to the wall so they don't tip. Curious animals tend to reach up and take a gander at what may be up on the shelves and are susceptible to falling shelves or cabinets! Treat and secure furnishings of this type as if you were protecting your two-legged toddlers. Protective railings are good and consider more wall-mounted items and less clutter. Place stuffed animal collections on more strategic shelving above windows or other cabinets—or keep them in inaccessible areas—they won't get into them as easily. For cats, I place objects close to the wall and not near the edge of shelving.

All windows, doors, and wall considerations are dependent upon what type of animals you have. Usually, these aren't a problem. Curtains can hold odors, dander, and claws of felines or canines, which can smell and be easily damaged or ripped. I recommend vertical blinds, (horizontal if high enough), smoked-glass shading, and protective screening on doors and windows to ease some of the curious jumping on and scratches may occur. Tough, stain-resistant, painted surfaces on walls that can be easily cleaned are a must. Fancy fabric walls and coverings are nice, but they are nicer to cats as scratching pads! Consider fancy paintings and wall coverings above chair rails where cats or dogs may not climb.

Cables and electrical outlets pose a hazard to our loved ones. Keep all cables covered, clamped close to walls, and preferably encased in protective covers. I keep them out of reach by mounting and tacking them securely against walls and corners—when feasible, I put them above the reach of my curious canines and/or felines. Strategically arrange cabinets and other appliances in front of sockets and outlets to help conceal and protect outlets, providing additional peace of mind. I limit the number of cables running through my house and use a lot of remote or cordless items!

Bathrooms are not a pretty subject, but we must bring up those sensitive areas. Some dogs love to drink from your "johns." If you use a bowl cleaner that sticks to the sides or put additives in your toilets, they may be toxic to animals. Put the lids down and keep those bowls cleaned thoroughly and flushed—and never use hanging deodorizers and cleaners. Some people keep lids up on clean bowls when away in case of storms. It may be an emergency avenue for dogs to get to water, but most will encourage folks to maintain their water containers and have them cleaned, filled, and changed at least once a day. If a storm is that large, the lid won't stay upright through the gusting weather anyway. There are also products that deliver fresh water. I also encourage guardians to clean out the water bowls beneath those automatic spouts because they still get dirty and grimy. Stagnant water can lead to many illnesses and bacterial infections. Never allow water containers to become grimy with algae and slime. Additionally, many people have bathroom products on sinks and on low shelving that dogs or cats can get into. Be wary of things in your bathroom that can injure or cause your loved ones to become ill. Secure items in cabinets and drawers if your bathroom door remains open.

Another area some may not think about is outside decking. Check your decking! Paws and legs can get caught in loose, damaged, or widely spaced decking. Check decks regularly for nails and screws sticking out as well.

Dogs love a lawn full of grass. Mine must have been cows in another life. Grass is a wonderful play area for your animal companions to frolic. Some eat grass for upset tummies so check your varieties. Some dogs have allergies so attempt to rid your yard of excessive weeds. Don't have your entire yard of grass where your pooches normally run. Let your dogs have an area to really mess up things. A sand or dirt area will satisfy bored dogs that want to dig and such. Unless you can constantly monitor hyperactive ones, you may find your yard and gardens in disarray. Consider fencing off your flower beds. Some plants are toxic and dangerous to your animals. Check with your local horticulturist for plants that are non-toxic.

Last but not least, I highly recommend **dog doors with an "attached-to-your-house" doghouse.** This promotes more security and would-be burglars may not know Brutus's doghouse leads straight inside your house! Attached doghouses will protect better in the heat and cold by giving a barrier between your house and the outside elements—and reduce the amount of bugs coming into the house. Make sure both ends have the **flexible** flaps to keep dogs from getting pinned. Never use rigid dog doors! Another great strategy is to place your dog door on the back of the house to minimize visibility from the road. Training your animal companions to go in and out of dog doors minimizes the chances of accidents on your nice flooring or furnishings. This gives your companions additional freedom, exercise, and chances to water your plants outside—especially when you're late and Skippy needs to really go!

The more of these things you have around your home, the more maintenance-free your domain will be from curious, hyper canines and felines in your lives. Supervision and frequent exercise are best for minimizing most problems. With hectic schedules, it becomes next to impossible to monitor our companions twenty-four hours a day. Your companion animal may need to be temporarily separated, contained, or placed in a more controlled environment for surgeries, training, or traveling. Crating dogs or cats because you're at work or for punishment should never be an option! If you need to keep a companion constantly locked up or contained, consider a new home for them that will be more suitable. You wouldn't want to live like that.

CHAPTER 19

Disaster Preparedness for Your Companion Animals

We need to be extra attentive to our wonderful canines as we endure unpredictable and adverse weather conditions. Though any month can be potentially irregular, spring and fall have always been known to bring about rough and ever-changing temperatures and conditions so we want to give humans some disaster preparedness tips for their four-legged family members. Your animals need to be a part of your disaster plans in the event of tornadoes, hurricanes, or other natural disasters. In the South, we have the ongoing threat of tornadoes and hurricanes.

Here are some things I do and some helpful ideas you can put into place to keep your animals safe:

- Include your animals in your disaster relief plans.
- Write a detailed plan with exits and shelter locations that include your favorite companions.
- Have sealed containers of water, food, and other animal items in your emergency kits—enough to sustain your companion as long as you plan to sustain all the humans in your household.
- Keep your companion's documentation and records handy to take along with your other important documents. You may store them in fire/water-resistant containers if you cannot take them with you. Some people have all records maintained on flash or jump drives to be readily accessible in any location.
- Keep all your all health and shot records up-to-date and on file at your local vet office.
- Have your companions micro-chipped if applicable and all current emergency contact numbers on file at your vet's office.
- Have a backup plan to temporarily house companions if needed with friends or relatives.
- Have easy escape routes for your animals.
- Dog doors are always a benefit for animals to quickly move out of harm's way. Have areas around your yard where your companions can easily run to for shelter and protection from outside elements.
- If in a flood zone, have elevated safe areas and shelters that your companions can easily access to be secure from drowning.
- Practice your emergency plans with your companions. They are, of course, part of your family. Have more a contingency plan and practice it on a regular basis.

- Post in a conspicuous area the number of animals—and pictures, if possible—with emergency contact numbers if you are not at home in the event of an emergency. Post this information on your front door and/or window. Consider putting this information in waterproof clear plastic so it can be read even if a storm passes through.
- Never crate a dog or cat at home alone! If an emergency arises, there is no way for your animals to escape.
- Have a companion-friendly neighbor or trusted friend keep an eye on your house when you are not home.
- Give them permission to remove your companions from your home in the event of any disaster with detailed instructions for special care or information about your specific animals.
- Certain animals have better survival skills than others. Consider these issues and tailor your disaster plans accordingly.

CHAPTER 20

Contingency Plans for the "Unthinkable"

No one wants to think about what would happen should you fall gravely ill or pass away. We need to consider contingency plans in the event that some drastic fate falls upon us. Think about your companion—and not yourself. Everything you do will have considerable affects on how your best friend(s) are treated should you be taken away from them for any reason. Several factors can come into play and adversely affect our animal companions in the process: unplanned moves, divorce, sudden death, illnesses, or incarceration. Let's take a look at a few suggestions to circumvent these tragedies and possibly make unexpected incidences smoother for our four-legged friends.

Since animal companions are not property, we need to consider their welfare in our long—and short-range plans. Longevity is indefinite; if something goes wrong, your animal friends won't end up in an abandoned home, starve to death, or be euthanized at the animal control center. If you consider your best friend as part of your family, you won't forget this important phase.

Long-term planning:

Always consider your domestic companion animals in your wills and declarations! Have a person or family declared a godmother, godfather, or contingency guardian who will ensure your loved ones will go on with adequate love and care in the event you die. Second, spell out specific guidelines on your financial terms that will provide for them without worry. Look into separate insurance plans if you can afford them. If not, are your heirs trustworthy to take on such an endeavor? Analyze your potential guardians of your animal friends before appointing them to this role. Are they equipped to take on such additions to their family? If your family of four-legged companions grows, modify your will accordingly to accommodate the changes. Take extra precautions as to how each will placed if there are requirements for them to be separated to different households.

Consider the contracts as seriously as you would your own. Don't haphazardly give this a fleeting second of your time. Take an extended amount of time when you consider the "who, what, and where" of the situation. The people you choose to carry on the role as guardians should have similar values and ethics to you. Ask and interview the prospective guardians of your intentions and make sure you know them as well as you think. Though Mr. Jones loves your two Schnauzers, Dexter and Daisy, he may not be so accommodating with Snuggles, your furry feline. Think outside the box and never be narrow in your thinking.

Your animal friends may be used to a particular way of life. Since each animal you have under your care may require different accommodations, environments, and guardians, try to be specific in your terms or have folks as heirs to your loved ones that have the same values as you do. Do your animals get along with other animals that may already live in that household? Does he or she have proper containment or dog doors? Have you considered the long-term financial requirements that will allow your companions nearly the same quality of life they had when you had them? No one will ever give your loved ones the exact same quality of care as you may have, but don't be overbearing on small changes. Slight modifications won't be traumatic on them if handled properly and if you've delegated someone who loves animals as well as you do, you should trust them to make the right decisions.

Give your prospective heirs documentation of your companions. If your animals are registered or entered into specific organizations, ensure they have all these (at least copies while you are alive) on each specific breed. Outline restrictions you may have. For example, if you have a young Doberman with his ears not cropped, you may, as an animal rights advocate or humanitarian, ask that they remain that way. Include spaying and neutering requirements, breeding, docking of ears, and cropping of tails. Ensure each companion is micro-chipped ahead of time in case they escape from their new guardians. And, they should know where to get the paperwork changed to reflect the new guardians.

If possible, allow your future guardians frequent visits, and perhaps dog-sitting to get to know their behavior. Birds, cats, ferrets, horses, pigs, and reptiles are unique in their behaviors; the best way for someone to get to know your animal friends is to meet them firsthand. If they are not available, communicate with them on a regular basis about your companions. This is especially helpful so you can know the character of whoever is taking care of them in the future. If you love your animals, take the time to get to know who takes your place. If your companions participate in some specialized programs, such as therapy dogs or seeing-eye companions, and your death occurs, keep their future guardians informed of your desires both verbally and in writing. Check with other activists or organizations for programs that may be in place should any ill fate come at any moment's notice. If they are a reputable organization and you've done your homework, you can feel comfortable that they will be provided for in the event of your passing.

All these hold true in the event of a permanent injury or illness. Situations of this nature may preclude you from properly caring for your companions for the rest of their lives in these instances. Humans call them living wills; remember to handle them in the same fashion as you would with the regular wills and contracts.

Short-term planning:

Some of the same rules apply in short-term planning as they do to long-term ones—with some minor adjustments. These plans ensure you get your babies back in the same condition and basic health as you left them (barring unforeseen accidents, etc.). Soldiers are frequently the ones to consider these plans. Also, those who take extended business trips or contracts overseas should take extra measures in considering temporary placements. Logically, these contractual agreements are modified according to length of time. Have your long-term plans ready in the event that things suddenly change.

Always have up-to-date records, shots, special medication instructions, and preparations in clear view for your temporary guardians. A good way to do this is to provide a complete copy of all your documents with them on a flash drive, disk, or hardcopy. All adoption papers, history, and pertinent information on your specific breed should be contained on them. If you are unsure of what to put on them, put it on there! Too much information is better than not enough. Go with your gut and your love.

If possible—and if finances allow—hire a sitter or nanny to be at your residence to avoid major movements during your extended stay or injury. An option could be someone staying almost rent free if they took on the additional duties as a nanny for your companions. You can come up with tailored agreements that will satisfy all parties if you sit down and take the time to brainstorm a few ideas. Two or more heads are better than one! Your local rescue organizations and animal welfare groups may have some publications or ideas on the matter and help you to come up with a specific plan as well.

Many groups, especially if you have been a longstanding member or financial backer, should give sound advice and assistance with your family's needs. Have several contingencies in place. Should one fail, you have a backup plan. Not everything goes as planned, but you can avoid major headaches and issues if you plan out as far in advance as possible. Again, no plan will be perfect, but you have to be willing to adapt. Their health and safety is your major concern. If you keep this in mind, it will work out for all parties involved.

Outline locations of your groomers, veterinarians, day care providers, etc. and try to keep the same humans involved in their care. You and your companions will become comfortable with them should this become a necessary practice. Temporary situations will go a lot smoother for them if you change as little as possible for them. Plan out your costs depending on your length of time away or set up an allotment or reoccurring payment plans to each facility that will be managing your animal's care. If there are no set facilities in mind, consider allotments to your short-term sitters for their care. Have some means of periodic monitoring their care and well-being—and where your money is being spent.

Don't go blind into a situation if something goes wrong. Have a secondary plan for that as well, such as a new location to transfer them and someone to call should this unforeseen event occur. Again, nothing is ever foolproof, but less harm comes to smart planners!

Technology is a fantastic tool at your disposal. There are several ways to keep up with your companion animals while you are on an extended stay. Cell phones, video-conferencing, and cameras are great tools. Utilize them to keep in contact and see and hear your animals interact throughout the separation. If need be, provide the temporary caregivers for your animals with an extra smartphone that might prove to be your savior. Always include them in your weekly progress reports or conversations while away. It will ease your mind in the long run and avoid sudden incidents that could have been avoided if you remained in contact with their care provider. Put as little of the burden of caring for your loved ones while away on the sitters as possible. If you went through all the planning and preparation to ensure your companions are in the best of care, you should always follow up! A plan can be great, but a watchful eye can be priceless!

Take into consideration that your companion animals should be afforded as much care to them in your planning as would a human child. This is obviously a given since those who have companions rather than pets have already considered the unconditional love between them and their furry and not-so-furry companions. Since people who love their animals want to provide for them in the best possible way, care should be taken in your short—and long-term contingency plans. Never throw an idea together without testing its validity. Consider dry runs or small trips to see how effective your plans are. Change as the situation or environment calls. It will save you time, money, and disappointments in the long run. Plus, your companions will be safer, well cared for, and less traumatized should the unexpected happen.

CHAPTER 21

Holiday Safety for Your Companions

When the holidays approach, be attentive to your animal companion's needs—safety should be top priority during these festive events. To get into the holiday spirit, get out stockings and fill them with doggy or kitty treats and toys!

Here are some safety tips that you should observe so you and your pampered pooches and kitties enjoy a stress-free and safe holiday season together! First, think safety for you and your companions during all your holiday preparations and decorations; it's really not nice to have such lovely decorations and find your canines and felines biting down on your holiday ornaments, etc.! Several safety issues should be addressed:

- Holiday attire: So many people want dress up their favorite pooches for the holiday. I find they come quite equipped with adequate clothing thus don't require this symbol of "vanity." However, if you feel you *must* do this, consider some simple guidelines. If you have well trained pooches or only a single dog guardian (the others will tear them off each other if untrained or overzealous), for very short periods of time, and only in supervised situations so they don't get tangled. Holiday attire has no benefit whatsoever for your companion; it is only for guardians' amusement and/or adoration. I don't do it and my dogs will tear them off in about three seconds anyway. As for humans and your holiday clothes, use common sense and don't have dangling things all over you that your dogs or cats can tear off and swallow!
- Stockings: Use stockings mounted high up and away from the fireplaces so your companions don't knock them into the fire! Mount them securely and away out of their reach! Have one for each family member, including all your four-legged or two-legged animal companions!
- Holiday snacks and treats: If you make treats for the four-legged babies, remember to feed in moderation and use healthy, animal-safe ingredients. Ask your vet for recommendations. You may want to try a specialty shop online or more reputable shops in your neighborhood. Just make sure they have your companion's health and nutrition in mind. If you don't, they'll have gassy, upset stomachs. For all your human treats that are unsafe for both canines and felines, remember to keep them out of reach and in secure

containers. If dogs or cats can smell them, they will try to get them. Be cautious and keep tasty but dangerous treats away from them. Don't eat treats in front of them unless you have some other canine/feline-safe treats in your other hand to feed them; it's not nice to tease! Try preparing additional holiday cakes or treats that you and Buster can enjoy during these festive occasions.

- Turkeys and hams: Do your best not to overfeed or even feed table scraps to your animal friends. We all have been guilty of this. If you do, consider very small amounts for this special occasion. Under no circumstances should you give turkey or chicken bones to your animal companions! They can pose a serious problem, such as splintering or getting caught in a dog's throat. Check with your local veterinarian about his or her thoughts about ham bones. I don't recommend any bones. If you are the parent of multiple dogs, they will definitely fight over them—no matter if you have one for each of them! Alpha dogs want all of them and will try to take them away from the others!

- Holiday lights, cables, and extension cords: Keep lights out of reach from Rover and Miss Kitty. Keep extension cords and other cords away from animal contact. Think fire safety at all times! Avoid situations where they may get strangled or electrocuted by the holiday trimmings or lights. Keep them hidden and attach them close along the corners and/or high above their reach.

- Holiday trees, wreaths, mistletoe: Holiday trees can pose unique problems to our animal friends. Just because your animal companions may not bother with trees outside (mine do if the branches are low enough) doesn't mean your tree is safe! Ensure live and artificial trees are non-toxic and securely mounted so they don't easily tip over. All decorations, trimmings, and wreaths should be safe and non-toxic just in case they get a hold of them—the same as if you were keeping things safe from your toddlers or grandkids. Never use additives that may be harmful to animals in the water troughs of your live trees. The best suggestions are fencing off decorated trees or never leaving your companions unattended. Don't forget that picket fences should never be used! Mistletoe can be toxic so be careful to keep your companions away from these items as well. Other holiday plants may be hazardous so check with your local vet.

- Outside decorations and ornaments: Never leave dogs unattended around your lavish decorations. If so, you just gave Brutus permission to have them as expensive chew toys. Also, some are made of glass, which can cut up a dog's esophagus and stomach lining if swallowed. Keep ornaments and holiday statues up high or mounted securely to the ground, safe from possible electrical shock, and non-toxic. Large Santa, reindeer, and Nativity sets should be staked securely in the ground so they do not tip over when curious pups investigate. Better yet, fence off or place in areas away from unsupervised areas. Picket fences are highly dangerous to dogs! Many medium and small dogs and cats may get pinned between the slats and choke! Avoid posts that stick up just above dogs extended stance or jumping heights if on a collar. If a dog comes down close to them, he or she might accidentally get caught on them and choke as well. Also a dog can get impaled accidentally—collar or not. Keep all fire hazards decorations out of the yard for you and your pet's safety. Take consideration of your cats also when decorating your yards if they are out as well.

- Holiday carolers: No one ever thinks of this, your lovable animal crew they may unintentionally scare off or intimidate friendly carolers that may come around this joyous season. I recommend placing a safety gate in front of the door in the evenings so when you open the door, your dogs won't immediately try to run out the door toward the nicely dressed people. Though you know it is because your hounds are happy to see them, the others don't realize this and your holiday carolers will be off to someone else's porch! Keep biters, including playful nippers, away from carolers. People love to sue these days! I also recommend stepping outside so that your dogs won't go crazy and interrupt the musical serenade!

I hope that this has given you some ideas to safely enjoy the holidays with your favorite four-legged companions. They are just a much a part of our family as the kids are so think of them during your holiday preparations this year. Keep all holidays safe and obstacle-free for your beloved animal companions!

CHAPTER 22

Working with Your Neighbors, Not Against Them

Through my many dealings within the community, I am approached by fellow dog lovers about how to confront a neighbor that may be suspected of mistreating or neglecting a family companion. We mistakenly want to react with aggressive and ineffective means. This particular article is directed to the not-so-severe cases only. There are several agencies, subject-matter experts, and publications available for serious situations. However, if you are in doubt, call your local animal control center or 911 for emergency situations! Let's look at just one example and find some proactive and preventative measures for ensuring a suitable quality of life for the pooch across the street, so to speak.

Case in point: You initially come upon your young new neighbor that has a somewhat skinny dog chained outside with no shelter and a water bowl knocked over and no chew toys.

Evaluate: Let us not forget that you need to be very certain of any accusations and the severity of situation(s). This means evaluate the situation first! How long has the dog been outside? Was the dog just placed there recently due to other reasons (repairs, awaiting containment, etc.)? Do you know the dog is being abused or neglected? Is this a case of overreacting by initial and distant observation on your part? Are you privy to all the facts—not mere assumptions? Did the neighbor across the street by some reason or another just inherit this unexpected pooch only moments ago and is uneducated on the proper treatment and care of this newfound friend? The dog may be a previous boyfriend or girlfriend's, their mother-in-law's, abandoned, etc. Too many people jump first and don't truly investigate. If the dog is in not as severe a situation as previously assumed, you should proceed to the next step.

Educate: Educate the neighbor with tact and positive motivational techniques. Some ideas could be dropping by and soliciting your services and expertise with assisting your neighbor or recruiting a fellow expert to handle it for you. By being inquisitive, using kind words, and tactically approaching the matter, you may find that the new guardian has just been placed in this newfound situation and has no clue of how to raise or protect the new roommate. Tread lightly and investigate, then give helpful solutions and aid where you can. Play an active role in helping with the construction of safe shelters or containment areas. Educate your neighbor on nutritional needs, socialization, and so on. Temporarily volunteer to assist during the down times or even while things are put into place for them. After these measures are taken, slack off on the involvement and observe from a distance.

Monitor: We want to monitor from a distance within reason, legal limitations, and with common sense. I want to caution the obsessive dog lovers though. The way others treat their animals may not be to your (even my) stringent standards but still be just as loving and appropriate. In other words, you may sleep with your dogs and other guardians have dogs sleeping outside that are just as loyal and happy as yours. Each situation calls for individual design as long as the physical, social, and mental well-being is accomplished between the guardian and their companion animals. I stress common sense and common rules. If you are not a subject matter expert, use caution when prejudging your neighbor's techniques.

Become a positive role model for your unknowing neighbor instead of becoming the neighborhood prude. Attempt to use positive steps before getting animal control or law enforcement involved. If it is truly just a neighbor who is simply ignorant and not abusive, work toward a more positive solution—do not become part of the problem. If you talk the talk, walk the walk!

In Summary: This advice is coming from an obsessive dog lover who took the long and arduous steps to learn self-control and not to jump to erroneous conclusions when I came upon some lean, dirty hound out playing in the yard that was actually a well-cared for pedigree simply taking a break from agility training events! Judge not your neighbor so harshly. You may not know everything! I literally had to keep my self-control and consider what was best for both parties. Through all of this, you may find the individuals in question are truly good people but were bombarded with a new resident they weren't ready for. Be part of the solution. Trust me, if they're not right for a dog, your last-resort options may have to come into play. Be patient. Evaluate, educate, advise, assist, monitor, and then reevaluate. Use animal control or 911 as an "imminent danger solution." Sometimes your animal resource center can offer assistance as a secondary resort on borderline cases as well.

CHAPTER 23

Canine Treats that "Make or Break" the Grade

Our Wooftips spy team reveals the real skinny on some of the common snack foods available to our canine companions.

We all love to give our favorite pooches a delicious treat when returning home from work or just seeing wonderful, loyal, smiling faces and wagging tails. Our team of doggy guardians from my previous network, Wooftips.com, and my current circle of friends (local and Internet/social networks) decided to looked at a few popular treats and give our unofficial rating on them. This is only a small group of snacks and there are hundreds of varieties that have come available for our companion animals. My advice is to look at the ingredients, consult your veterinarian for what snacks and rate of consumption is best for your particular companion's needs. Lastly, always look on the back of each package and look for primarily natural ingredients with low salt and sugar!

Our WoofTips Scales

- 4 or 5 smiles—Tastes were overall great and humans rated them great.
- 3 smiles—Good, but not as good/limited intake/tastes varied
- 1 or 2 smiles—Not recommended for a variety of reasons

 Type Treat: Chicken jerky treats by Wagon Trail and Milo's Kitchen

Commonly found: Large chain superstores
Our comments: Great snack; we give them a "five." Made of all-natural ingredients and doesn't add all that salt. Though moderately expensive, they are well liked/digested by the canine crew of the family! Great for medium to large dogs. Not recommended for small or toy breeds unless you break them into smaller pieces.

Type Treat: Dog treats by Milo's Kitchen

Commonly found: Large chain superstores

Our comments: Great snack, we give them a "five," but they are going to cost if you have multiple dogs in the house. Dogs really like the taste of these and digest them quite well. Guardians tend to overdo the giving on these so consider rationing. Made of all-natural ingredients and doesn't add too much salt. Great for all dogs sizes, but you will need to break up some of the varieties.

 Type Treat: Active PrePro Biscuits by VitaLife Plus

Commonly found: Large chain superstores

Our comments: Great snack. We give them a "four" only because the dogs prefer the meaty products but seem to take these well. They are fortified with vitamins, which gives added kudos. Made of all-natural ingredients and doesn't add all that salt. Less expensive, they are liked and digested by the canine members of the family! Great for medium to large dogs. Okay for small breeds if you break them up; easy to break apart.

Type Treat: Homemade dog treats from recipes or specialty shops

Commonly found: Home, Internet, books, specialty stores, etc.

Our comments: These were normally good reviews. Some still had high fat content and low nutritional value. Some of our test subjects really didn't like a few of them so guardians have to find ones that their particular four-legged companions favor. Guardians need to be cautious about ingredients that may be allergy inhibitors, and/or high in calories. Consult your vet if your dogs require particular foods. Our test dogs experienced a lot of excess gas though it seemed to settle down after a period of time—even with the online natural treats that were found at gourmet specialty shops. We found if they tasted good to us, usually Bowzer seemed to like them. Be careful and read all the ingredients and consider reputable, well-known distributors. Making them yourself can be a great sense of joy but again, note fat and nutritional values. Limit the snack intake to avoid pudgy pooches! Overall, we'll give them a "four."

Type Treat: Bone marrow treats by typical name brand sources

Commonly found: Large chain superstores, many other local stores

Our comments: We've found about half of our dog candidates didn't really go for them. Although some had real bone marrow, they weren't wolfed down like some of the other treats. We give them a "three." Nutritional value was dependent upon the brand name and typically had very low percentages. These were relatively inexpensive and usually had sizes to fit most breeds.

	Type Treat: Dog biscuits by typical name brand sources **Commonly found:** Large chain superstores, many other local stores **Our comments:** Though these were relatively inexpensive and usually had sizes to fit most breeds, we found that dogs were mixed in their likes and we usually didn't find one particular type that was appealing to our entire test pooches. We had to go through several types to find one that didn't have enormous fat content or ingredients that show little or no nutritional value(s). Going with the higher end or more natural products, we give them about a "three" as well.
	Type Treat: Imitation bacon strips **Commonly found:** Large chain superstores, almost everywhere **Our comments:** Not our favorite snack, we give them a "two." They are very high in fat and have useless ingredients. The disadvantages clearly outweigh the benefits. The smell is great, but the taste is nothing like bacon! A lot of people like these though. If you do give them, we recommend limited quantities due to high fat content and they do not digest them well. You'll have more waste outside if you give them a lot of these snacks. Just like cheap dog food—more goes out of the dog—but the fat starts weighing in as well!

	Type Treat: People food snacks (Hot dogs, pizza, bologna, etc.) **Commonly found:** home **Our comments:** We don't like overall, but dogs absolutely love them. Be cautious about what types of food you are giving your treasured one. Usually, these treats, even in limited quantities, have very low nutritional value, high fat content, have common allergic reactions, upset dog stomachs, common gas, and have other health issues. Dogs aren't made like us. Also, we tend to overfeed little Muffy and you end up with pudgy Muffy. If you give your dog people food, be very cautious, and limit the intake! I've been guilty of this—as we all have—but I've truly lessened my temptations and it's been far better for my bunch! We are not speaking about specific recipes people prepare for natural feeding, such as raw diets. There are wonderful holistic and natural recipes some will spend the time and money on.
	Type Treat: Pig ears **Commonly found:** Everywhere **Our comments:** Not a good choice. Highly susceptible to bacterial growth if not digested the same day. Also, they have a tendency to get filthy since dogs tend to carry them all over the house and yard. No nutritional benefit although dogs seem to enjoy them physically and emotionally. These treats are only geared toward larger dogs and are not recommended for smaller or toy breed dogs. We give them a "one."

Type Treat: Rawhides

Commonly found: Everywhere

Our comments: We give them the same rating as the pig ears. We really don't recommend them. Additionally, they are not very digestible, have zero nutritional value, and can be dangerous to some dogs. Staying away from them altogether is our comment! Dogs usually love them, but guardians need to be cautious. We highly recommend close supervision if you give them to your dogs. Also, we found dogs to continuously fight over them if they were alpha dogs. Definitely not a recommended treat to give to small dogs either!

Checking in with your veterinarian and reading package labels are great deciding factors on your choice of doggy snacks. Some dogs are more finicky and it may take a few tries to figure what he or she likes. Additionally, though some of these specialty shops sell many different treats, check their ingredients. Some dogs may be allergic to certain ingredients; others are quite healthy, but your pooch may not desire them. I ordered some specialty treats from a friend's gourmet shop, but my dogs didn't like them. Go for a small amount first. Never buy in bulk until you know your favorite companion likes them. For multiple dogs, attempt to find their unique preferences because—like humans—not all dogs think alike!

CONCLUSION

If you take only a few helpful tips away from this book, always remember that companion animals should never be regarded as mere property. Humans should start moving toward managing their lives to show that we consider these animals to be a part of our family network. In this book, I wanted to work toward readjusting your attitudes when it comes to domesticated animals and I hope you will progress in your way of thinking and consider them living, breathing, non-human animals that require understanding, intervention, and attention.

I have experienced these instances in prevention, maintenance, and care with the countless dogs I've cared for and through the many families I've assisted throughout the years. This is an ongoing commitment—and I still must practice and follow these tips I've put together for you with my own four-legged crew. These recommendations have been tried and tested by average dog guardians. We've all learned a tip or two from mistakes and, unfortunately, we've also had some losses. Let's do our best to minimize these for everyone's concern. Dogs, like any domestic companion, are brought into your family network by choice! No one wants to lose his or her loved ones due to human error. Consider your companion's needs each and every day.

As always, you should consult with your veterinarian for any health-related issues. You may also wish to get second opinions from other reputable organizations on overall animal welfare. Everything can be relative and subjective. The primary goal is to focus on the animal's well-being and quality of life with you or your family in a peaceful and humane coexistence. This is the twenty-first century—we must upgrade our attitudes and technology in regard to improvements in an animal's quality of life. Activists and guardians are always looking for ways to humanize how our companion animals live. All companion animals should be allowed to live in humane fellowship while we protect, supervise, and care for their daily needs. It was man that altered and genetically re-engineered those who were once wild, creating the domesticated animal that depends on our protection. It is our responsibility to love, defend, and provide for them throughout their existence.

Don't Leave Them Out . . .

- of your holiday festivities. They've been there patiently through all your trials and tribulations the entire year round. Even when you ignored them on occasion, they wagged frantically and let you know they still love you

- in the cold. You wouldn't want to be stuck there either. What if it was you shivering from the cold and rain? Provide safe, adequate shelter for companions that ask for very little in return.

- on a chain. Solitary confinement—on a chain or in a crate—for extended periods creates undesirable behavior patterns. Dogs (and cats) have feelings and they can be mentally and physically harmed when chained and/or crated for long periods of time.

- dumped alongside the road or abandoned. You took in this defenseless creature, promised to give him/her a home and as soon as your situation changes, he or she is the first to be abandoned. Please consider them as an extension—not a liability to your family. Puppies grow up and suddenly the "cuteness" goes away or they become more of responsibility than one perceived. You wouldn't leap into adopting a child—so why do so when adopting a four-legged friend?

- and not report abuse. It is our responsibility to report and prevent abuse. If you see or suspect abuse, please report the incident to animal control! If they find it was not abuse, you still took the precaution and were a watchful and caring citizen. Animal abuse is many times a precursor to other abuses—don't let it go unreported!

- in an open bed of a pickup truck, unsecured or unprotected from the elements. There are specific regulations for how a dog should be tethered in a pickup truck. By following those guidelines, your best friend won't be injured or thrown from the vehicle—or killed by another driver. You may be a safe driver, but the other guy may not be! Plus, a safe driver would not allow his best friend be subjected to such dangers. Not only is it unsafe—it is against city ordinances to have a dog improperly placed in the back of a pickup truck! Animal control can help you with the proper techniques for tethering your dog safely. They have all the details if you call them. Report others that break these laws as well!

- of your social calendar. You entertain the guests that arrive for the holidays, but we tend to forget our animals when we have additional guests in the house. Many times, the dog is put out when guests come. If your guests are allergic or cannot manage with your best friend there, then take some separate time and spend it with your companion! He did no wrong! He came to your family in hopes of finding true companionship and love—not a temporary fix from loneliness until someone else comes around! Dogs (and cats) really do show love and loyalty. If given a chance, they will be a joy throughout the year—and not just a seasonal commodity!

V. Nunley

Save a Dog from . . .

- **Shelters . . .** lonely, confined, and in need of socialization; desperate for human companionship and compassion.
- **Chains** . . . neglected, abused, vulnerable to elements and attacks with nowhere to run for protection from harm.
- **Confinement** . . . crated and caged for hours on end, forgotten and regarded as property with no real place to call home or a real someone to call friend.
- **Dogfights** . . . cruel, abusive, and immoral, yet practiced widely and ignored by many who consider themselves citizens of the community.
- **Puppy mills** . . . sold off as a commodity—a thing used for profit—and living in constantly dismal conditions.
- **Ignorance** . . . the uneducated and the unwilling humans who see their dogs as property— it denies dogs the right to a better quality of life.
- **Extinction** . . . a life deprived of natural instincts to roam, socialize, and play; a desire to be characterized as a dog and not a showcase for self-serving human vanity.
- **Inhumanities** . . . exploitation, marketing tools, and public spectacles—marked only for status, ratings, financial investment, or profit margins.

V. Nunley

"No reason but for vanity/profit for humans to continue senseless breeding of domesticated animals!

Blinded, for they don't see the millions of homeless animals when the breed they seek awaits adoption!

The abandoned ask only for a chance at survival; prove humanity is not so vain and self-serving."

V. Nunley

Never compromise on companion care!

The End